MINNESOTA SYMPOSIA ON
CHILD PSYCHOLOGY, VOLUME 2

MINNESOTA SYMPOSIA ON CHILD PSYCHOLOGY

Volume 2

JOHN P. HILL, EDITOR

THE UNIVERSITY OF MINNESOTA PRESS • MINNEAPOLIS

BF
721
.M545

Library of Congress Catalog Card Number: 67-30520

PUBLISHED IN GREAT BRITAIN, INDIA, AND PAKISTAN BY THE OXFORD
UNIVERSITY PRESS, LONDON, BOMBAY, AND KARACHI, AND IN CANADA BY
THE COPP CLARK PUBLISHING CO. LIMITED, TORONTO

Preface

In May 1967 the Institute of Child Development was pleased to welcome to the University of Minnesota the participants in the second of its annual Minnesota Symposia on Child Psychology. Their papers are published here and, as in the first volume of symposium papers, are meant to inform the reader about programs of research. Each investigator was asked to talk about his own research program and to provide his own interpretative framework for it. Although we had no general theme in mind in selecting participants for this symposium, a careful reading of the volume suggests a leitmotif of concern with structure. Whether some subtle bias against functionalism was operative when we selected participants or whether we have sampled the zeitgeist representatively, structural themes, explicit and implicit, appear and reappear within the otherwise diverse papers in this volume.

In a time when research on personality development is dominated by the study of processes of social influence, it is important and refreshing to have some conceptually sophisticated work on personality structure. Unlike the older predeterminist approaches to structure which hatched gaggles of traits and little else, the interactionist view taken by Wanda Bronson promises more productive outcomes. Using the data of the Berkeley Guidance Study, she has identified two dimensions of personality, Emotional Expressiveness–Reserve and Placidity-Explosiveness, which are central (account for much of the variance in multivariable intercorrelation matrices) and stable from childhood through adulthood. Each dimension is seen as one manifestation of a larger cluster of behaviors resulting from a corresponding and underlying orientation. Orientations are "characteristic and unmodifiable predispositions to certain modes of interaction." Bronson has employed a construct validation strategy to adduce meaning for the dimensions and their corresponding orientations. Although cultural myths, peer response, and parental values are seen as interacting to reinforce or modify preferred patterns of behavior, the question of the origin of orientations is left open.

The "I to III" of Brown, Cazden, and Bellugi-Klima's title, "The Child's Grammar from I to III," refers not to age but rather to periods of early language development for which the authors are writing generative grammars. The grammars are written to represent a child's knowledge of language structure at a given point in time. Such representations already have proved to be a remarkably useful tool in comparative linguistics and have great promise for major advances in our understanding of the nature of language development. Brown and his associates are conducting a longitudinal study of the development of grammar in three preschool children. Transcriptions of the spontaneous speech of the child and the mother in conversation provide the primary data for the study. The portions of the research program reported here call attention to the hypothesis that the development of grammatical competence is innately programed, to the distinction between grammatical knowledge and performance, and to some other phenomena that are the stuff of current controversy between learning and cognitive partisans.

One of the costs of an experimentally oriented science is the absence of information about the nature of freely varying behavior as it occurs within freely constituted environments. To make the collection of such information one's objective is to invite onerous problems of data collection and data reduction. In this volume we are introduced to APPROACH, A Procedure for Patterning Responses of Adults and Children, devised for ecological research by Bettye Caldwell and her associates at Syracuse University. The standards set for the development of this system were stiff ones: applicability of a computer-compatible coding system across age, number of interacting persons, and situations. Summaries of APPROACH records are presented for five children of different ages so that the reader may judge the potential of the system for ecological research. Although such a system has utility for the solution of many kinds of problems, Caldwell is interested particularly in using it to explore the relations between individual development and the structure of environments in which learning takes place. For example, the system gives promise of being useful in the solution of applied or evaluation research problems. Comparisons of the outcomes of experience in Environment A with Environment B always will be uninformative to social engineers without behaviorally relevant ways of describing the environments involved — whether A and B are specified as Freudian and Skinnerian, Traditional and Montessori, or ghetto and suburban.

Hershenson argues that developmental psychologists have paid little attention to the effects of cognition on perception. In his research on that topic, the stimuli employed are English words of varying approximations to the letter frequencies and sequential dependencies of English. Such structural differences in the stimuli are taken to reflect varying orders of conformance to the structure of English as it is represented in S's memory. The data suggest that the more closely a stimulus approximates the structure in memory, the better it is perceived. Hershenson considers information-processing models to provide the best theoretical leverage for the discovery of the mechanisms underlying this effect and other effects of cognition on perception in children and adults.

The Austin–Mexico City project is a large-scale, cross-cultural longitudinal study of cognitive, perceptual, and personality development being carried out under the direction of Wayne Holtzman and Rogelio Diaz-Guerrero. With Jon Swartz and Luis Lara Tapia, they present in their paper some of the results for the first two years of the project. The data reflect central, and what may turn out to be stable, differences in styles of coping behavior between the children in the two cultures. The American children approach the assessment situations more actively. They seem more direct and forthright in their approach to problem-solving, more venturesome, and more willing to risk failure. The Mexican children approach the same situations more passively, tend to respond in terms of immediate sensory experience, and give evidence of less highly differentiated cognitive and perceptual structure. How these differences hold up over a greater time span remains to be seen, but the results thus far are consonant with other observations of differences between the two cultures. The care taken in sampling (through the use of cross-national matching), in reducing examiner variability, and in assuring linguistic equivalence of meaning in the test materials make this project a methodological exemplar for cross-cultural research.

Many persons and organizations helped bring about the symposium and this volume. Dr. Zofia Babska of the University of Warsaw presented a paper but unfortunately was unable to prepare it for publication. Financial support came from Public Health Service Research Grant No. HD-01765 through the National Institute of Child Health and Human Development and from the research funds of the Graduate School, University of Minnesota. The faculty and graduate students of the Institute of Child Development and colleagues from other institutions helped at various stages in the process of selecting participants. Institute faculty members consulted about editorial matters. Competence, support, and unflappability once again characterized the work of the staff of the University of Minnesota Press throughout the editorial and production process. The greatest indebtedness is to the psychologists whose good work provided the occasion for this symposium and whose good nature made arranging it and editing this volume a pleasant responsibility.

JOHN P. HILL

Magnolia, Massachusetts
December 1968

Table of Contents

MINNESOTA SYMPOSIA ON
CHILD PSYCHOLOGY, VOLUME 2

◈ WANDA C. BRONSON ◈

Stable Patterns of Behavior
The Significance of Enduring Orientations for Personality Development

DESCRIBED in operational terms, my research activities of the past few years have consisted in, first, identifying behavior patterns that remain both stable and central from childhood through adolescence and, second, determining what characteristics of the individual and of his environment come to be associated with such patterns at different stages of development. The findings established in the course of this research have led me to propose that two dimensions of behavior, Expressiveness-Reserve and Placidity-Explosiveness, are manifestations of what may be called orientations; that is, characteristic and relatively unmodifiable predispositions to certain modes of interaction which play an important role in determining the nature of the individual's experience, his effectiveness in coping with developmental tasks, and the kind of beliefs about himself and others that

NOTE: Were it not for the cooperation of the subjects in the Berkeley Guidance Study and the dedication of Jean W. Macfarlane and her staff who, over the years, studied the subjects' development, none of my analyses would have been possible; my indebtedness to them goes beyond any expression of gratitude. I wish to thank all my colleagues for their contributions to my investigations; I should especially like to acknowledge my debt and gratitude to Marjorie Honzik for the judicious admixture of criticism and support she was ever ready to offer, to Brewster Smith for his most helpful comments on the lucidity of my presentations, and to Joanne Mechanic for her invaluable mediation in computer analyses. Norman Livson, a steadfast friend and critic, was in addition a valued collaborator in the early analyses and decisions about selection of the pool of behavior ratings and in the establishing of developmental periods. Part of the work on which this report is based was supported by Public Health Service Research Grant MH 06238-02.

he eventually comes to maintain. I use the word *orientation* in preference to any other because I should like to avoid at present all theoretical connotations about nature or origins, such as have accrued to more familiar concepts — for example, that of temperament. Detailed reports on various aspects of my investigations have been published (Bronson, 1966a; 1966b; 1967). In this paper, I shall rely mainly on summaries of findings most relevant for documenting my position, illustrating the steps by which it has emerged, and elaborating its implications.*

My research has not developed from any well-articulated theory. Its main impetus came from the challenge inherent in the data of the Berkeley Guidance Study, the challenge of arriving at a meaningful framework within which over thirty years' observations of development could be analyzed. Three of my long-standing convictions have supplied the direction of research and are among its major themes. First is the belief that to understand the meaning of any particular event fully, it is necessary to appreciate its history. Second is a concern with the concept of consistency — a search for some formulation in which the requirement of demonstrable continuity in observed behavior would not preclude recognition of dynamic equivalence among disparate behavioral manifestations. Third, there is my own predilection for hypotheses relating persistent individual differences to nature as well as to nurture.

All my analyses use data collected in the course of the Berkeley Guidance Study, a longitudinal investigation of the physical, mental, and personality development of persons selected to be representative of the population born in Berkeley, California, in 1928–1929. Although the socioeconomic range in the composition of the sample is substantial, the

* Readers interested in a more detailed presentation of analyses and issues summarized in this paper will find "Central Orientations: A Study of Behavior Organization from Childhood to Adolescence" (Bronson, 1966a) a source for all questions relating to the method by which the dimensions were originally defined and proposed as manifestations of enduring orientations. The investigation of factors in the early life of the child (his behavior, mental development, the family milieu) which relate to behavior on the two dimensions in later periods is described and discussed in "Early Antecedents of Emotional Expressiveness and Reactivity-Control" (1966b). "Adult Derivatives of Emotional Expressiveness and Reactivity-Control" (1967) is the reference for the study of relations between childhood and adolescent position on each dimension and personality at age thirty. An unpublished manuscript contains a number of investigations: the replicability of the dimensions, the generalizability of the model, the relation of the dimensions to contemporaneous school behavior, social attitudes, peer and parental relations, as well as the issue of covariation with physical attributes, both early and contemporaneous, are taken up in detail and characteristic patterns of correlates are discussed.

majority of families from which the subjects originated are white, middle-class protestants. The stresses the subjects experienced in growing up were neither much more nor much less than those experienced by most such groups in the United States during this period. The sample has been followed from birth to adulthood under the directorship of Jean W. Macfarlane, who published (1938) a detailed statement of the goals of the study and of many of the methods used in collecting and codifying information. Although the nature of the sample in the Berkeley Guidance Study necessarily imposes certain limitations on the generalization of findings, restrictions differ according to the kind of inference that is made; discussion of this issue will become more relevant as the main points of the argument are developed.

The main body of my research concerns a group of forty-five boys and forty girls, all members of the extensively studied guidance group of the Berkeley Study, selected to include all subjects who had been seen continually between the ages of 21 months and 16 years. An investigation of the evolution and development of enduring traits requires that the sample be constant; ideally, the functioning of the same individuals should be described at different times and in different situations. This requirement could not be strictly met in the present case: the scope of the Guidance Study precluded the possibility of ensuring that all observations of all subjects would be obtained at all times. The selection of the core group was a compromise designed to reconcile the conflict between the requirements of size and constancy of sample. Even though the criterion of continuous participation does not guarantee that all data are available for all core subjects at all times, it does ensure that only minor variations in group composition occur in any given analysis. In socioeconomic terms, the core sample is no different from the original sample of the Berkeley Guidance Study; comparisons of core and non-core subjects along various measures show no indication of bias; as far as I can ascertain, the only feature unique to the core group is its consistent participation in the study.

The bulk of my analyses involves the time span between the ages of 5 and 16. For a variety of reasons — primarily to simplify conceptualization and to increase reliability of measures as well as availability of subjects — the conventional chronology of yearly intervals was not followed. Instead, the 12 years between ages 5 and 16 were divided into four periods of 3 years each: early childhood (ages 5, 6, and 7), late childhood (ages 8, 9, and 10), early adolescence (ages 11, 12, and 13), and late adolescence

5

(ages 14, 15, and 16). Ratings repeated at intervals within any period are generally averaged into a composite score; it is over those four periods that stability is defined and the main analyses of change and continuity are sought. I have also referred to information obtained during two other periods of life and related it to findings obtained within the main time span; these are the preschool period (3½ years or younger) and early adulthood (30–33 years).

For information within the main time span I have drawn primarily on four sources: (a) ratings of the subjects' behavior made by the caseworker on the basis of all available information; (b) codifications of teachers' observations of behavior in the school situation; (c) measurements of physical and mental development; and (d) ratings of parents' behavior and of their relationship with the child. Despite my emphasis on longitudinality, on occasion I have made use of information available for only one period rather than all four; this partly reflects a particular interest in self-report data and scores not mediated by a rater's judgment. During the preschool years, information about the child's behavior is limited, but detailed assessments of family situation and physical and mental development allow some description of the subjects' functioning. To investigate adult outcome, I have used an overall assessment of personality represented by a hundred-item Q sort, based on information obtained in the course of a series of extensive interviews with the subjects.*

To arrive at the concept of orientations, it was first necessary to establish that there are behavior patterns both enduring and central over time. For source data, I turned to the caseworkers' descriptions of the behavior that characterized the child at each of the four main developmental periods. These descriptions, expressed on scales well defined by explicit behavioral cues, represent a variety of statements that the interviewers considered both useful and important to make in their assessments of the subjects' development. Although not exhaustive, the scales sample a wide spectrum of behavior and allow for an adequate description of the individual's main modes of functioning. From the over fifty variables rated at one time or another by the caseworkers, I selected thirty-five that (a) were used for at least half the period between the ages of 5 and 16 and (b) permitted reasonable within-sample discrimination at all ages.

* The adult personality Q sorts, based on the California Q deck (Block, 1961), are from a major project under the direction of Jack Block and Norma Haan (Block & Haan, in press).

The stability of behavior as assessed on any scale is expressed by the persistence of ratings over time at any given level; it is indicated by the degree of correlation between ratings on the same measure obtained on any two separate occasions. By centrality I mean the power of a given variable to predict position on other variables. On the assumption that the more predictive the variable, the stronger and more numerous will be its correlates, I used the sum of squared correlations (Σr^2) of a given variable with all other variables in the matrix as an index of its centrality.

For each of the thirty-five scales, both the degree of centrality at each period and the extent of stability over the four periods were computed. The two sexes were treated as separate groups in this and subsequent analyses. I was left with a problem of applying my criteria to the results: given the variation in centrality at different periods, in stability at various transition points, and in results characterizing the two sexes, what measures can qualify as being, on the whole, most central and most persistent in the development of boys and girls alike? With the aid of plots and distributions I arrived at a scheme by which all the measures could be fairly and clearly ranked in terms of the centrality and stability shown over the developmental span in both sexes. From within the top third of variables best fitting my requirements two clusters of scales emerged, both of which could be established as tight groupings at each period and in both sexes. The first cluster — the variables Expressive-Reserved, Gay-Somber, and Shy–Socially Easy — constitutes the proposed dimension of Emotional Expressiveness–Reserve. The second cluster — the variables Phlegmatic-Reactive, Calm-Explosive, and Compliant-Resistive — forms the proposed dimension of Placidity-Explosiveness.

The results of this analysis are basic to the methodology and conceptualization of all research which followed. The two dimensions are the main tools used in all my subsequent analyses of behavior organization. The adequacy and validity of the model I use depends to a large extent on the replicability of these tools, on how universally the measures used in defining each dimension represent interrelated observations of behavior that is both enduring and predictive. Since the Berkeley Guidance Study included in its design a second sample, referred to as the control group, a limited cross-validation study was possible. Certain differences between the guidance and control samples limited the scope and interpretation of this and other attempts at replication of issues raised by my research: the control group had minimal opportunities for personal discussion with the staff;

7

information about behavioral development in the control group was obtained largely by a single caseworker; ratings of the behavior of the children in the control group reflect the mothers' unedited reports rather than the considered clinical judgments of the Guidance Study interviewers to whom a variety of sources were available.

Despite these differences in data collection, a number of identically defined scales were used in recording the behavior of both groups, and thus an analysis of persistence and centrality of various measures similar to that undertaken with data from the guidance group was possible. The findings were essentially replicated: imposition of the two dimensions on the matrix of behavior ratings of the control group does not violate the requirement that the definers of each dimension be among the most central and persistent of the behaviors assessed; the dimensions again represent tight groups of measures interrelated at all periods and for both sexes; as dimensions, they are both central and enduring.

Both persistence and centrality are relative concepts. The correlations descriptive of the stability of the dimension of Emotional Expressiveness–Reserve from any one period to any other, established in both the guidance and the control groups, vary around a median r of .70; those descriptive of the persistence of the dimension of Placidity-Explosiveness have a median r of about .50. Within each period the two dimensions together exhaust over half the variance residing in the matrix of all correlations among the various ratings of behavior.

Let me clarify the relation between the dimensions and the proposed orientations, the predispositions to certain modes of interaction. The dimensions reflect one aspect of what I believe to be a far larger cluster of characteristic behavior resulting from the particular orientation. At any given developmental stage or in any particular group, the two dimensions may not necessarily be the best, the most "core" manifestations of the orientations; however, their attributes of stability and consistent centrality allow the construction of an empirical framework for the investigation and better definition of the underlying orientations. In the model I propose, the dimensions serve as guidelines; it is the analysis of their correlates that gives evidence of the nature and evolution of the orientation.

In applying this model, I have assumed that the most essential characteristics of the particular orientation will be suggested by those variables that correlate significantly with the dimension at all four periods and among boys and girls alike, that is, from correlates established irrespective of time or sex. I limit the description of such correlates to those obtained in the guidance group: Although a large number of associations are found to replicate in analyses of control group data, the differences in the nature of the material from which the dimension scores arise require that instances where replication cannot be established be analyzed carefully, with emphasis on the extent to which the fact that the control group's behavior is viewed by mothers and the guidance group's by clinicians may be responsible for differences in results. Such analyses are complex, laborious, and result in statements which still remain somewhat equivocal. For the present, I should say that the nature and extent of both similarities and differences in correlates of the two dimensions as established in the guidance and control samples vary as a function of age and sex of subject, but that substantial agreement on characteristic interpersonal behavior can be established. I believe that such discrepancies as do occur can be reasonably understood to reflect the differing perspectives of mother and clinician and do not contradict the main inferences about the nature of the orientations.

To be significant, a correlation in the guidance group has to reach a minimum strength of .30; the associations I describe vary from this minimum level to correlations as high as .70 or .80. Rather than list variable names I shall illustrate the kind of behavior the particular orientation implies by resorting to the descriptive statements which correspond to high and low numerical ratings along the continua most consistently associated with a dimension. Children and adolescents who are spontaneous in expressing their feelings, feel at ease in most situations, and are usually lighthearted and gay — that is, children who score high on the dimension of Emotional Expressiveness–Reserve — are described by caseworkers as characteristically aggressive in social situations: They try to dominate their group and enjoy being the center of the stage. They are responsive to the demands of the external situation and easily accept the values and codes of the group; they rarely appear anxious and show a matter-of-fact acceptance of their own proficiencies and deficiencies. They are restless, they tend to move and fidget constantly even when engaged in engrossing activities. Their teachers describe them as always willing to participate in things, as being friendly and outgoing, spontaneous with everybody, emotionally an open book. They are cheerful and full of fun, quick to joke and responsive to humor. They tend to be the leaders in their class and will usually try to dominate the situation; they find it somewhat a strain to accept suggestions.

Conversely, children and adolescents who score at the other extreme of this dimension — who never give full expression to their feelings, experience acute discomfort in all social interactions, are serious-minded, and take life heavily — are described on other continua as retiring, passive participants, content to follow or submit to others; they are more responsive to their inner feelings than to social codes. An undercurrent of worry seems to be characteristic; they are vulnerable to criticism, lack humor, do not seem to enjoy themselves. They do not care much to make friends at school, they engage in little social life, and are markedly reticent about themselves. They are inactive and prefer sedentary occupations.

In these descriptive statements, I see two themes merging to define the nature of the orientation: one suggests differences along a continuum ranging from ebullience to depression, from an overflowing of high spirits to a flat, heavy, constricted affect; the other points to differences in the extent to which interaction with other people, whether in personal or social relations, serves as a focus of involvement.

To turn to the second dimension, Placidity-Explosiveness, and the orientation it implies: Children and adolescents who are calm and not easily upset, who are pliable and docile, whose anger reactions are mild or practically nonexistent — that is, children who score high on placidity — are described by caseworkers as somewhat stolid. They run on an even keel and considerable provocation is needed to shift their prevailing mood. They try to avoid friction and seldom quarrel; explosions, and even milder reactions such as crying or whining, are rare. Characteristically, they are sound, quiet sleepers.

Conversely, youngsters who score toward the explosive end of the dimension — who are tense and easily stimulated, resistive and argumentative, and for whom anger means near total loss of control — are described as volatile, characterized by frequent though not persistent ups and downs, depressions and elations. Little antagonism or frustration is needed to provoke them to quarrel, their explosions are not only severe but also frequent. They complain often and overtly, and their sleep is restless and disturbed.

Here again two themes are merged: one relates to differences in readiness to react, in degree of prevailing tension; the other implies a concomitant characteristic tendency to contentiousness or, conversely, to phlegmatic or even propitiatory behavior.

I have limited the discussion of the dimension of Placidity-Explosiveness to the consistent correlates from within caseworkers' ratings. In the first two childhood periods, that is, during elementary school years, teachers' judgments reflect the image implied by the descriptions I have just quoted: The child who scores toward the placid end of the dimension tends to be pliable in school, he fits well into class routines, he seldom misbehaves. He appears calm and stable; he is a child who prefers quiet activities. Conversely, the child scoring at the explosive end of the dimension will tend to be resistive and stubborn in school, one who frequently upsets class routine. He is tense and easily annoyed, his behavior is fidgety, he is often found out of his seat. However, by the time subjects reach junior high school and, even more so, senior high school, their position along the dimension of Placidity-Explosiveness shows little relation to behavior characteristic in the school situation. Teachers' ratings express a strong and consistent agreement with caseworkers' views on what characterizes children who differ along the dimension of Emotional Expressiveness-Reserve, and strong associations with measures relevant only in school suggest the extent to which the orientation has a uniform impact on behavior in a variety of situations. The dimension of Placidity-Explosiveness is not only less strongly and pervasively correlated with teachers' ratings during the childhood periods but seems to lose most of its relevance for school behavior in adolescence.

I stress this difference in pattern of school correlates of the two dimensions because it illustrates more clearly than other analyses what I consider to be a meaningful difference in the nature of the two orientations. Although I maintain that both are enduring and relatively unmodifiable tendencies to certain modes of interaction, the behavioral expression of the orientation defined by the dimension of Emotional Expressiveness-Reserve is more pervasive, that of Placidity-Explosiveness more selective, particularly with increasing age. In more concrete terms, I suggest that in a given interaction it is more possible to stimulate or provoke a child who generally tends to be placid-controlled to reactive-explosive behavior or, conversely, to impose calmness and control on one who tends toward reactivity and explosiveness than it is to inhibit that child's expressiveness or break through his reserve.

Consistently nonsignificant, near-zero correlations established in both sexes between the dimensions and other measures further illuminate the nature of the two orientations by reflecting some things that they are not. The two dimensions are not correlated — they remain consistently orthogonal throughout development, and their correlates generally arise from different areas of behavior. The few descriptions common to both orientations are those implying differences in level of activity: both expressiveness and explosiveness result in more active behaviors than do reserve and placidity. Judgments based on less extensive and less articulated observations than those made possible by the caseworker's involvement with the subject can easily reflect this communality and generate dimensions that are not so clearly independent. With ratings such as those available for the guidance sample, the type of activity associated with each dimension can be differentiated. Stated in terms I have used earlier in the discussion, it is clear that ebullience may be associated with over-reactivity, but it need not be, any more than involvement with people need be accompanied by contentiousness.

My investigation of the relation between position on the two dimensions and assessments of physical characteristics of both guidance and control subjects have led me to conclude, although tentatively and with qualifications, that physical attributes are not an important determinant or derivative of either the orientation implied by Emotional Expressiveness–Reserve or of that described by Placidity-Explosiveness. Whether this kind of relation exists is an important issue: Whenever the question of enduring personality traits arises, there is a strong temptation to turn to hypotheses of biological determination, or at least reinforcement. Since differences in patterns of social behavior, particularly those characteristically associated with differences along the dimension of Emotional Expressiveness–Reserve, have been shown to be associated with differences in physique by other investigators, perhaps most notably by Sheldon, the issue becomes particularly relevant to all speculations about the nature and effect of at least one of the orientations with which I am concerned.

My qualifications stem first from the fact that the physical givens I have investigated are limited to anthropometric measures and indices of maturation rate. Broader, more sophisticated measurements might have detected areas of biological contribution that I could not establish. Second, although they are specific to one sample, or one developmental period, or one sex, instances of significant covariation between physical attributes and position on the dimensions do occur in the data. Different connotations accrue to the two dimensions depending on the age and the sex of the child as well as on whether the clinician (guidance group) or the mother (control group) is viewing behavior, but on the strength of the whole body of my findings I believe that the orientations inferred from the dimensions share substantial similarity across samples, time, and sex. In my view, which certainly may be disputed, acceptance of a hypothesis of biological contribution implies a certain inevitability of association: relatively minor differences should be overridden, and both persistence of association over time and replication (at least within one sex) need to be established.

In the guidance group, the only significant association found at all periods and which shows at least tentative replication on control sample data indicates that boys who score low on the dimension of Emotional Expressiveness–Reserve, that is, who are somber, shy, and withdrawn, are rated higher on the somatotype component of ectomorphy than their more expressive peers. The only other consistently significant correlation, between high scores of placidity and weight, is characteristic only of boys in the guidance group and is not replicated in the control group. For girls, no persistent associations with physical characteristics can be established in either sample.

Although the specificity of associations between the two dimensions and the assessments of physical characteristics leads me to argue against a hypothesis of basic biological contribution, findings of covariation of certain behavior patterns with certain physical characteristics, even if of limited duration, are nevertheless significant in a different context. At the period when it prevails, such covariation may be one of the factors which contribute to determine what particular social responses are evoked by the child and thereby act to modify both his contemporaneous behavior and subsequent development of his personality. I turn now to the general issue of social reactions and consider first some of the main differences in the effect that the two orientations appear to have in the course of development depending on whether the child is a boy or a girl.

In the main, the correlates of the dimension of Emotional Expressiveness–Reserve are quite similar in the two sexes; there are few statistically significant sex differences in strength or in direction of correlations with other measures. However, over many analyses, there have emerged a number of slight but persistent and internally consistent differences in the degree to which certain measures are associated with the dimension in each sex. Overall, they suggest that for the boy, behavior arising from an orientation implied by high scores of expressiveness is generally admired and evokes affection, thereby representing a consistent source of inter- and

13

intrapersonal success. Very similar behavior on the part of a girl evokes a more mixed response: to put it most succinctly, she appears admirable but somewhat off-putting. What is at issue, I believe, are the qualities of assertiveness and of interpersonal salience that are inherent in the orientation. Since they are congruent with the image of dominant masculinity, they are ego-syntonic to the boy. Insofar as they conflict with the stereotype of the properly feminine, they lead the girl to oversensitiveness about issues of power; her behavior—perhaps defensively—becomes more domineering, her sociability more manipulative and less genuine.

Since this distinction between the sexes has evolved on the basis of evidence that relies primarily on consistency of various results internally and over time, it is difficult to document without adducing large quantities of data. However, by citing some specific findings from analyses of a social attitude questionnaire, I can at least illustrate my position. The questionnaire consists of items drawn from the Ethnocentrism (E), Authoritarianism (F), and Political-Economic Conservatism (PEC) scales reported in *The Authoritarian Personality* (Adorno et al., 1950). It was administered to Berkeley Guidance Study subjects in late adolescence when the social behavior associated with the dimension of Emotional Expressiveness-Reserve is, as is true also in other periods, substantially alike in boys and girls. However, the responses to the questionnaire indicate that the two sexes differ in a number of social attitudes associated with position on the dimension. Among the most marked differences is that the more expressive the girl, the more she subscribes to attitudes denoting political and economic conservatism; the more expressive the boy, the more he rejects them. (This sex difference in direction of correlation between the dimension and the PEC Scale remains highly significant when socioeconomic class is partialled out.) Further, the more expressive girls tend to agree with statements such as "No weakness or difficulty can hold us back if we have enough will power" (F Scale) and "The trouble with letting Jews into a nice neighborhood is that they gradually give it a typical Jewish atmosphere" (E Scale), whereas the more expressive boys tend to disagree; the differences in direction of association are strong enough to be statistically significant. Despite similarities in overt interpersonal behavior, the presence of these differences in social attitudes confirms the impression that the orientation acquires a different meaning in the course of development of the two sexes, and their nature is congruent with the view that the expressive girl's friendliness and sociability are bound more by power

14

considerations and hence are less genuinely loving than are the expressive boy's.

From the same perspective of socially approved stereotypes for sex-appropriate behavior, it is hardly surprising that a tendency to placidity or to explosiveness in a boy would have a different impact and acquire a different meaning than the same tendency in a girl. Data from a "Guess Who" sociometric technique administered in junior high school shows that the more placid the girl, the more frequent are her classmates' votes claiming her to be "most popular." This does not hold true for the boy. After early childhood, instances of significant sex differences in correlates of this dimension are generally more frequent. The overall tenor of associations indicates that, for the girl, an orientation of placidity is accompanied by self-reliance; that her behavior, though contained, is comfortable; that her interactions are matter-of-fact but not strained. For the boy, a number of significant changes in direction of correlates of the dimension occurring between childhood and adolescence suggest that an orientation of placidity is associated with a pattern of increasing withdrawal over time, of generalized cautiousness, and of a passivity with overtones of immobilization. On the social attitudes questionnaire, again there are significant sex differences in beliefs expressed by adolescent boys and girls with similar scores of Placidity-Explosiveness. Among girls, there is an apparent congruence between their placid or explosive behavior and the attitudes to which they subscribe: the weltanschauung of the placid-controlled girl emerges as more acceptant, easier, gentler than that of her reactive-explosive peer. Among boys, however, there are instances where the attitudes they endorse appear to be at variance with their characteristic behavior. For example, "An insult to our honor should always be punished" (F Scale) is a statement with which, as would be expected, reactive-explosive girls agree with more than do placid-controlled ones. For boys, the correlation is in the opposite direction; this somewhat belligerent attitude is endorsed more strongly by placid boys, whose behavior tends to be placating, than by explosive boys who generally behave far more contentiously. To abstract a judgment of conflictual or, conversely, conflict-free functioning: being expressive or reserved, or being placid or explosive, appears to carry different connotations for the two sexes. A rather direct covariation with adaptiveness is inferred with Emotional Expressiveness–Reserve among boys and with Placidity-Explosiveness among girls; however, in the reverse instances (Emotional Expressiveness–Reserve for girls, Placidity-Explosiveness for boys), the relation is not a simple one since position at either extreme appears to create problems of adjustment.

In discussing the role that the orientations play in the course of boys' and girls' development, I have focused on cultural expectations as an important factor in determining what is appropriate and therefore ego-syntonic. Clearly, the nature of the response from the most immediate environment, the family, is an important source of support, modification, or compensation for views that the child develops from others' responses to his characteristic tendencies. Since I believe that what is probably most important is not *what* the parent does but how or why he does it, I have relied heavily in this area of my investigations on patterns of covariation and subsidiary analyses of selected groups. These data need extensive presentation to be fully evaluated. Consequently I shall report here only the most explicit findings.

For both boys and girls the dimension of Emotional Expressiveness–Reserve is relatively independent of parental behavior; the orientation is apparently maintained as a characteristic style irrespective of family attitudes. It is generally true that an expressive mode of behavior, whether son's or daughter's, is associated with maternal warmth and ease of relationship; conversely, strain and a certain distance characterize the interaction between mother and reserved child. For both sexes, the mother's behavior would seem to reinforce the prevailing pattern on this dimension: her friendly ease with the expressive child can enhance his outgoing attitudes; her strained distance with the reserved child may push him even further into emotional withdrawal. In the case of girls whose expressive, outgoing tendencies appear to result in behavior which evokes a somewhat ambivalent social response, the support of a good relationship with the mother may also represent an important source of strength in coping with the reflected image. Correlations with assessments of paternal behavior are generally not significant. However, since I have in an earlier report (Bronson, 1966b) expressed my belief that identification with a strong same-sex parental model is one of the processes that facilitates the development of an expressive orientation, I was unwilling to accept at face value the lack of significant associations between the father's attitudes and the son's behavior. More detailed analyses of distributions of covariation on some of the measures of father-son relationship did give at least tentative evidence that the lack of significant correlations is due perhaps more to a bimodal relationship, either very warm and friendly or very strained and hostile, between father and the highly expressive son than to a real lack of predictable associations between fathers' attitudes and sons' tendencies toward emotional expressiveness or reserve.

The degree of association between parental attitudes and the child's Placidity-Explosiveness is relatively strong; sex differences in the magnitude of correlation with various measures suggest ways in which parental behavior either reflects or contributes to the differences in the development of the orientation in boys and girls. The strongest and most persistent correlations are established with the boy's behavior: The family milieu of the placid boy is consistently marked by marital harmony between stable and calm parents; the son's relationship with both mother and father is consistently supporting and satisfying. Here the orientation of placidity finds rewards not accorded by peers; whereas reactive-explosive behavior, admired by schoolmates, is met with parental disapproval.

The total family atmosphere and the boy's own behavioral tendencies mutually reinforce prevailing patterns, a complementarity which is less marked among girls: the daughter's tendency toward explosiveness or placidity appears to reflect far less directly the behavior characteristic of her parents. There is an indication of change in maternal attitudes toward daughters over time: the mother's easy but somewhat distant relationship with the placid daughter in early childhood becomes warmer and more companionable by adolescence, in contrast with a growing impatience and strain with the reactive girl as she grows older. The best and perhaps most significant illustration of the difference in mothers' attitudes toward Placidity-Explosiveness in sons and in daughters is that, throughout most development, mothers tend to overprotect their placid sons but urge independence and responsibilities on placid daughters. (Since this information comes from correlational analysis, it is well to remember that the passive components of the son's placidity may as easily result from maternal overprotection as cause it.)

I have tried to illustrate the meaning that the orientations assume during the child's development by describing patterns established in the periods of childhood through adolescence and by focusing on the child's sex as a major factor that creates a different social environment in response to similar behavior. An additional level of complexity is introduced when long-range rather than contemporaneous effects of the orientations are taken into account. Correlations between position on the dimensions attained at various developmental periods and adult outcome, assessed at about age thirty by Q sorters totally ignorant of early case history, show that the role of the orientations in shaping adult personality is a function not only of sex but also of age. It is important to understand the mechanics by which such age-differential prediction from persistent ratings is possible: Although the orientations are relatively stable throughout development (that is, it is probable that a youngster described as expressive in childhood will be also judged as expressive in adolescence) a certain degree of variation in scores on each dimension does occur over time. A period in which behavior characteristic of the orientation is particularly intense may be followed by one in which it is less strongly apparent; the youngster who ranked first in his group in early childhood may rank tenth or fifteenth by late adolescence. It is such age differences in dimension scores that allow for the emergence of adult associations of differing degree. The variation in scores may be a result of chance factors, it may reflect error of measurement, or it may indicate that meaningful change in the constellation of contemporaneous tasks and past experiences is occurring. I shall lay this issue aside for the moment to outline briefly the main patterns of prediction of adult outcome.

No matter when his behavior along the dimension of Emotional Expressiveness–Reserve had been assessed, a boy whose scores were toward expressiveness will tend to become a warm, likable, gregarious man. The extent to which this dimension predicts adult outcome (i.e., the number of its correlates) increases with age of assessment. High scores obtained by a boy during adolescence predict additionally that as a man he will be productive and not anxious, insightful and gay, dependable and self-assured — in other words, a man characterized by a generally high level of psychological functioning. Apparently the cumulative experience of inter- and intra-personal success that accrues to those boys who are able to maintain, or to develop, any inclinations toward an orientation of emotional expressiveness results in extensive internalization of attitudes leading to adult effectiveness and competence. Conversely, an orientation of reserve maintained throughout the formative years is increasingly detrimental to successful adult outcome.

The long-range effects of Emotional Expressiveness-Reserve in girls are rather different. High expressiveness scores at all developmental periods predict characteristically assertive behavior in adulthood: it is the quality of interpersonal salience rather than interpersonal warmth which achieves the most consistent long-range stability. In addition, one set of adult characteristics is predicted from Emotional Expressiveness–Reserve rated in early childhood and another set from the same dimension rated in late adolescence. Associated with girls' expressiveness in early childhood are adult characteristics such as rebelliousness and self-dramatization, a lack of control and of genuine dependability — accompanied, however, by self-doubts about personal adequacy. Highly expressive behavior in late adolescence predicts a poised, gregarious, and cheerful woman who is, however, moralistic, conventional, and given to projecting her own motivations onto others. I have suggested earlier that position at either extreme of the dimension comes to create its own difficulties for the growing girl, and indeed, the adult outcome predicted from girls' late adolescent expressiveness is more difficult to subsume under simplistic judgments of psychological health or disturbance such as can be applied to the adult personality of expressive or reserved boys. Comparison of prediction from childhood and adolescence does suggest, however, that girls who remain highly expressive throughout development or who by late adolescence come to manifest more fully their expressive tendencies are able to reconcile successfully, if not ideally, the conflict between their assertive disposition and social expectations.

Turning to the second dimension: For boys, a tendency toward placidity at all periods is reflected in adult stolidity, conformity, and over-control. Again a pattern of differences emerges over time, one set of adult characteristics is predicted from both of the childhood periods, another from both of the adolescent assessments. The adult correlates characteristic of early and late childhood placidity elaborate themes of both interpersonal and intellectual constriction and suggest some degree of retained immaturity. I refer here to judgments such as "does not have a wide range of interests," "prides self on being objective," "not changeable in behavior and attitudes," "has repressive tendencies," "uncomfortable with complexities," "creates and exploits dependency in people." Boys who remained or became more placid in adolescence are considered in adulthood to be genuinely dependable, to behave in a manner consistent with their own standards, not to be self-indulgent, to tend to ruminate and have persistent, preoccupying thoughts; overall, this is a judgment of productive, if perhaps compulsive, functioning. As noted earlier, the pattern of correlates contemporaneous to the ages at which the dimension was assessed suggests that, for boys, the impact of the orientation changes in the transition from childhood to adolescence. This change appears to be reflected,

19

too, in the reported differences in prediction of adult outcome. However, I had inferred that an increasing level of difficulty was associated with a placid orientation, an inference which does not seem quite congruent with the generally happier adult outcome predicted from dimension scores obtained at the later, adolescent period. It is perhaps here that the effects of a consistently supportive relationship with the parents comes to play a role, allowing the boy to achieve eventually, if not contemporaneously, a reasonably successful adaptive mode.

Among girls, early adolescence is the only period from which a significant relation between level of Placidity-Explosiveness and adult outcome can be established. If in early adolescence the girl's behavior is characteristically placid, as an adult woman she will tend to be judged as calm, relaxed, intellectually alert, and socially charming — a generally likable, competent, and successful person. Conversely, of course, characteristically explosive-reactive tendencies during this period are prognostic of quite seriously unsuccessful adult outcome.

The fact that the predictiveness of the dimension, though significant, is limited in girls to only the early adolescent period is intriguing. Patterns of correlations between assessments of this dimension over time and other contemporaneously assessed variables indicate that uniquely at preadolescence the placid girl is judged more physically attractive than a girl of reactive tendencies, that her achievement in school is, at that time only, significantly greater. Uniquely during the daughters' preadolescence, mothers of placid girls are rated as more stable themselves; in their relationship to the daughter they are at their most companionable. Hence, a girl's orientation of placidity seems particularly rewarding to her at that one period. Additionally, of course, the period of early adolescence is also marked for the majority of the girls in the sample by menarche, an important developmental event. In trying to understand why early adolescence should have the characteristics of a "sensitive" period as far as adult outcome of earlier tendencies to placidity or explosiveness is concerned, I should rely on inferences resulting from juxtaposition of all these findings. The girl who, for whatever reasons, is able to meet the crisis of her own womanhood with all the attitudes which distinguish a placid orientation — calm, self-reliance, matter-of-factness — and who also finds a source of support in her relationship with her mother, blossoms out during this period and the experience, whatever subsequently occurs, is material in affecting her eventual competence. In proposing such an interpretation I am suggesting that one of the distinctive features of this, and perhaps of all developmental crises, is that it results in an increased sensitivity to specific factors that neither before nor after are of particular import.

Throughout the discussion of adult prediction I have implied my conviction that the changes in predictive patterns are not a matter of chance but, rather, that they reflect the ever-changing interaction among characteristic tendencies, social valuations, parental supports, and developmental pressures. My position is somewhat paradoxical: on the one hand, I point to the persistence of ratings along each dimension over time as evidence of the enduring quality of the orientations they describe; on the other, I stress whatever variation in dimension scores does occur as a potential source of valuable information about changes in meaning and function of these stable orientations. Throughout I rely on consistency of findings more than on statistically significant differences, a procedure open to much justifiable criticism. However, I believe suspending disbelief and pursuing hypotheses that follow from acceptance of such findings are worthwhile, since they may lead eventually to formulations articulate enough to allow both methodological precision and conceptual complexity.

The proposition that the two orientations represent enduring tendencies toward certain modes of interaction, whose behavioral manifestations become characteristically attenuated or exacerbated at different periods of development with consequences important for subsequent outcome, focuses attention both on the reasons for the stability of such behavior and on the factors underlying the changes in intensity or overtness of their manifestations.

It is clear that in certain instances the tendency toward a particular orientation is highly gratifying: the consistent success of a boy's expressive-outgoing behavior is a good example. However, the equally consistent lack of success which follows from a boy's orientation toward reserve acts only to reinforce his withdrawal rather than to modify his behavior, suggesting that factors other than contemporary social rewards must be operating. In this context, assuming that some persons may inherently be more likely than others to vary in all areas of behavior, I have pursued the possibility that a tendency to greater or lesser stability in behaviors subsumed by the dimensions may reflect individual differences in a general factor of lability. Since lability of scores on one dimension (defined as the sum of squared deviations from the subject's own mean score over the four periods) is found to be independent of lability of scores along the other dimension, and since both are equally unrelated to lability in other developmental measures (of IQ or of physical development), such a possibility seems unlikely. I have also found no evidence that changeability along the dimensions is related to any greater frequency or intensity of disruptive events in the child's life than is stability. If, as seems reasonable, factors other than contemporary pressures contribute to the stability of the orientations, the focus naturally turns to the characteristics and events in very early periods of life.

My attempts to establish possible antecedents of the two orientations have been very limited — at the present stage of my research I can go little beyond speculation and programmatic statements. I have investigated some of the early characteristics of the child and of his environment that can be shown to relate to later position along each dimension. Operating within a limited universe of early factors, I have established that gross variation in physical development, either at birth or in infancy, does not seem to bear any consistently significant relation to the dimensions. Mothers of children who in later years score toward the expressive end of the first dimension and the explosive end of the second one report more problem behavior at about two years of age; correlations with various assessments of the early family milieu suggest that the parents of such children have a generally higher level of responsiveness, activity, or reactivity. However, the available observations are too gross and occur too late in the life of the child to allow me to elaborate on hypotheses of genetic contribution, such as have been raised in this context by studies of twins, to furnish information on the nature or stability of infant precursors of later Emotional Expressiveness–Reserve or Placidity-Explosiveness, or to contribute evidence on the question of whether such predispositions are innate or develop at some more or less early stage in response to environmental events: I enumerate these possibilities here merely to indicate the general direction of my future research.

What I consider the most important theme to emerge from my investigation of antecedents of the two dimensions is also the most tantalizing one, since it relies on complex juxtapositions of a large number of patterns and requires extensive longitudinal data for replication: this is the overall finding that the significance of antecedent relations I have established varies with the age at which the orientation is being assessed in later life and with the sex of the child; in many instances, the changes in patterns of antecedent conditions parallel the changes over time in the adult derivatives of the dimensions. Findings of such parallels both lend support to the hypothesis that changes in dimension scores are due to more than chance factors and allow for some exploration of what processes may be contributing to increase or decrease in intensity of manifestation.

Let me illustrate one such complex of patterns by referring to analyses of the dimension of Placidity-Explosiveness in boys. As I have pointed out earlier, a set of measures persistently associated with the dimension defines the orientation throughout the boy's development as one of calm and docility at one extreme and contentiousness and tension at the other. Simultaneously, correlates which change in degree of association between early childhood and late adolescence suggest that an orientation of placidity becomes increasingly associated with generally passive behavior and decreasingly with ratings from which a degree of self-acceptance or confidence can be inferred. The adult derivatives of childhood placidity differ from those predicted from adolescent placidity: adult constriction and immaturity characterize the former; productive, if compulsive, adult functioning characterize the latter. I cannot find any major changes in the nature of environmental pressures or supports surrounding the placid boy throughout development: the calm family atmosphere and supportive attitude of both parents are similar in the placid boy's childhood and in his adolescence. My own analyses of peer reaction are limited, but in his studies in reputation, Tuddenham (1951) concludes that "traits connoting docility and unassertiveness tend to be rejected . . . this pattern is stable over a considerable age range." I therefore infer that perhaps the most significant developmental difference may be that by adolescence the persistence of the placid boy's experience, both positive and negative, may have had cumulative effects on his self-perceptions. In the context of all these findings, the fact that the character of the antecedents of Placidity-Explosiveness in childhood is different from that of the orientation as manifested in adolescence assumes particular significance. A tendency toward placidity during the boy's childhood seems to derive primarily from an early peaceful situation created by the interaction of a quiet, easy toddler and a calm, stable, somewhat submissive mother in an atmosphere of parental and conjugal affection. By adolescence, the significant early predictors of the dimension lie mainly in the father's behavior during the child's earliest years: a close and affectionate relationship with a generally warm, outgoing father marks the early experience of the placid adolescent boy.

Two notions with implications that go beyond this particular example arise from such juxtaposition of findings. First, even though each finding of correlation pattern can itself be assigned no more than marginal significance, the fact that a substantial number of different assessments follow an identical pattern over time suggests that sheer chance is an improbable and insufficient explanation. The possibility of contamination within the data arises here: Blunt critics of longitudinal studies have suggested that regularities among observations established by this method may reflect more what is in the observer's mind than what characterizes the subject's behavior. In the pattern I describe, judgments made of the subjects in adulthood are exempt from possible halo effects, since they were made with no knowledge of the previous case history. I cannot rule out contamination in all other observations; I should merely point out that a large number of different caseworkers would have had to share an identical view of development and to be capable of remembering and interrelating a vast quantity of information over a long period of time in order to create this pattern — this possibility appears rather unlikely.

Second, the pattern suggests that the orientation evolves from a relatively simple to an increasingly complex response. In childhood periods, an orientation of placidity or of explosiveness appears to reflect rather directly the ease or strain of both the earlier and the contemporaneous situation; the adult derivatives suggest that the long-range effects of a seemingly ideal absence of early strain may, in this instance at least, act to limit the full complexity of which the organism is capable. The patterns of the adolescent periods suggest that accommodation is now being made to a much wider environment, which includes valuations of the culture as well as of the immediate milieu. The quality of the early father-son relationship is increasingly important as the boy himself approaches manhood: In the subjectively defined environment of these later periods there seems to be a merging of cumulative effects of past experiences, contemporaneous pressures, and ideas about the future. Although not surprising, it is important to research on this subject to realize that the longer the history of the evolution of the orientation, the more complex the nature of its determination will be.

A brief evaluation of the research I have outlined will serve as my conclusion. In common with others, I follow an interactional model in the study of development: The phenotype is defined as arising from interaction between the genotype and the environment; observable personality is seen as a system of traits, behaviors, affects, and attitudes evolved by the individual in a continuous process of coping, within the limits of his capabilities, with the tasks of his own life. The interactional process is continuous from conception to death. Throughout, the genotype, which merely sets the broad limits and perhaps determines preferences, is modifiable by experience; experience, in turn, varies in its nature and in its effects depending on the nature of the genotype. I use *genotype* in its analogous sense, to refer to something which I consider fundamental, rather than in its technical genetic meaning as pertaining to heredity. Although there has been growing evidence of a genetic component in the determination of at least sociability (see, for example, Freedman's (1965) beautifully controlled longitudinal study of identical and fraternal twin infants, which demonstrates a significantly greater concordance in intensity of social orientation and fear of strangers to characterize identical twins) and my own bias is toward accepting hypotheses that invoke constitutional differences as one of the factors contributing to stable orientations, I do not feel justified at this time in going beyond the limitations of my data.

Set in terms of this interactional model, the study of continuity in personality development requires units of analysis that would encompass the interactional process, since, by definition, persistence on the purely phenotypic or purely genotypic level is not possible. It is here that the concept of orientation achieves its value: different, yet rationally interrelated phenotypes are subsumed within a genotypic predisposition (postulated as such because of its enduring and pervasive character), whose manifestations, impact, and meaning evolve over time as a function of the ongoing experience it is itself instrumental in shaping. In my view, perhaps the main strength of my research is that it illustrates this approach and some of its potential value.

As for the two specific orientations I propose, my level of confidence in their validity is relatively high. It is reassuring to find that the framework of two dimensions as persistent manifestations of stable orientations could be replicated in a second group whose experience did not include that element of caseworker intervention which is unique to the guidance group and which is neither replicable nor of known effects. Beyond the limits of the Berkeley Guidance Study samples, factorial studies of personality have generated dimensions not inconsistent, even if admittedly not identical, to those I have proposed. For example, it has been pointed out by Adcock (1965) that Eysenck's factor of Intraversion-Extraversion and Cattell's

25

of Exvia-Invia are essentially in agreement; both share with my dimension of Emotional Expressiveness–Reserve connotations of differences in sociability and in degree of inhibition. Further, Adcock suggests that Eysenck's second factor, Neuroticism, as well as Cattell's Anxiety can be reconciled under the name of "emotional reactivity," which, in turn, bears much resemblance to my dimension of Placidity-Explosiveness. Equally, it is reassuring that the main consensus of longitudinal studies lies in findings of persistence of behaviors quite similar to those I rely upon (Honzik, 1964) and also that it is widely accepted that individual differences in sociability, irritability, reactivity, and activity can all be established at very early stages of development, even if their stability or the manner of their transformation into later, more complex responses is not as yet well documented. Although not definitive, different findings converge to establish the case for the existence of stable and central patterns of behavior, which, whether defined in precisely the same terms I use or not, are at least not inconsistent with the dimensions I propose. All of them reflect profound differences in interpersonal modes and would necessarily create a different environment for subsequent development.

I am far less certain whether the particular course of development found to be associated with the two dimensions in the guidance group is replicable or to be generalized. I have postulated that the evolution of the orientation arises from the continuous interaction between genotype and environmental factors; these latter are all intricately bound with culture. Social standards will differ from group to group, from one decade to the next, and the family, peer, and social sanctions or pressure met by Berkeley Guidance Study subjects around World War II may not be characteristic of any other sample or period. Nevertheless, even if their situation were unique, I believe that to chart the course of their development remains of value, first, to demonstrate that interaction does exist and, second, to suggest parameters which, *mutatis mutandis*, should be universal. Among these, age and sex emerge as critical elements in all interactions, insofar as they both evoke a different social response and define constitutional differences. Age also implies differing amounts of previous experience brought in by the individual to define the subjective environment in which the interaction takes place. Cultural myths, peer response, and parental values all interact to support or modify the individual's preferred modes; the process of internalization of others' views emerges as a highly significant factor in the evolution of the orientations. Only in one instance

— in discussing preadolescent Placidity-Explosiveness in girls in relation to their adult outcome — have I referred to the specific life task in which the individual is engaged as an important factor entering the total interaction. Although I have not isolated other such tasks for consideration, it seems obvious that what the individual has to achieve, at whatever level of conscious endeavor, is bound to be affected by and, in turn, to affect the orientation with which it is approached.

References

Adorno, T. W., Elsa Frenkel-Brunswik, D. J. Levinson, & R. N. Sanford. *The authoritarian personality.* New York: Harper, 1950.

Adcock, C. J. A comparison of the concepts of Cattell and Eysenck. *British Journal of Educational Psychology,* 1965, 35, 90–97.

Block, J. *The Q-sort method in personality assessment and psychiatric research.* Springfield, Ill.: C. C. Thomas, 1961.

———, & Norma Haan. *Ways of personality development: Continuity and change from adolescence to adulthood.* New York: Appleton, in press.

Bronson, Wanda C. Central orientations: A study of behavior organization from childhood to adolescence. *Child Development,* 1966a, 37, 1, 125–155.

———. Early antecedents of emotional expressiveness and reactivity-control. *Child Development,* 1966b, 37, 4, 793–810.

———. Adult derivatives of emotional expressiveness and reactivity-control: Developmental continuities from childhood to adulthood. *Child Development,* 1967, 38, 801–817.

Freedman, D. G. Hereditary control of early social behavior, in B. M. Foss, ed., *Determinants of infant behaviour III.* New York: Wiley, 1965.

Honzik, Marjorie P. Personality consistency and change: Some comments on papers by Bayley, Macfarlane, Moss, Kagan & Murphy. *Vita Humana,* 1964, 7, 67–72.

Macfarlane, Jean W. Studies in child guidance. I. Methodology of data collection and organization. *Monographs of the Society for Research in Child Development.* 1938, 3, 6, 1–254.

Tuddenham, R. D. Studies in reputation III. Correlates of popularity among elementary-school children. *The Journal of Educational Psychology,* 1951, 42, 257–276.

◈ ROGER BROWN, COURTNEY CAZDEN, AND ◈
URSULA BELLUGI-KLIMA

The Child's Grammar from I to III

A GROUP of us at Harvard are engaged in a longitudinal study of the development of grammar in three preschool children. One of the children, Eve, is the daughter of a graduate student, Adam is the son of a minister who lives in Boston, and Sarah is the daughter of a man who works as a clerk in Somerville. Eve's and Adam's parents have college educations; Sarah's parents have high school degrees. The principal data of the study are transcriptions of the spontaneous speech of the child and his mother (occasionally also the father) in conversation at home. For each child we have at least two hours of speech for every month that he has been studied; sometimes as much as six hours. Sarah's records are entirely transcribed in a phonetic notation that includes stress and intonation. The other children's records are not in phonetic notation except at a few points where some particular hypothesis made the notation necessary.

Figure 1 identifies an initial developmental period which has been the focus of our analyses thus far. The initial period has been defined in terms of the means and ranges of utterance length, terms external to the grammar. The period begins, for all three children, when the mean was 1.75 morphemes and ends when the mean was 4.0 morphemes. The longest utterance at the lower bound of the interval was 4 morphemes; at the upper bound, 13. Mean length of utterance is useful as a rough term of reference for developmental level in this early period but it grows more variable and less useful with age.

NOTE: This research was supported by Public Health Service Research Grant MH-7088 from the National Institute of Mental Health.

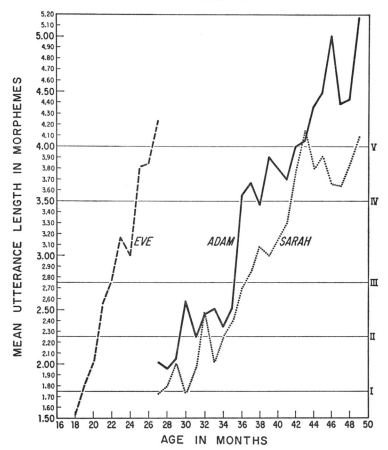

Mean utterance length and age in three children. The horizontal lines I–V represent five points for which generative grammars are being written.

As can be seen from the figure above, the children were not of the same chronological age when the study began: Eve was eighteen months; Adam and Sarah were twenty-seven months. We selected these three children from some thirty considered on the basis of matched initial performance rather than age. At the end of the period for analysis, Eve was twenty-six months, Adam forty-two months, and Sarah forty-eight months. In terms of the utterance length the rates of development of the three children may be ordered: Eve, Adam, Sarah.

The research is directed at two general questions. What does the child know of the structure of English at successive points in his development?

By what processes does he acquire his knowledge? The most explicit, comprehensive, and systematic form in which adult knowledge of grammar has been represented is the generative transformational grammar (Chomsky, 1957; 1965). A generative grammar is a system of rules that derives an infinite set of well-formed sentences and assigns them correct structural descriptions. The most demanding form in which to pose the question of the child's knowledge of structure at any time is to ask for a generative grammar that represents his knowledge. We are attempting to write such grammars for the three children at each of five points in the initial developmental period. These points are marked with lines and Roman numerals in Figure 1; they fall at nearly equal intervals across the period. For the grammars we make detailed distributional analyses of seven hundred utterances from each child.

A complete annotated grammar is between fifty and a hundred pages long, and so none is presented here. We do, however, present portions of a single grammar, the one written for Adam at III, to illustrate the kinds of knowledge such a grammar is designed to represent. Then, using Adam III as a kind of temporary terminus, we provide a descriptive overview of developments in the first period. Following this we offer more detailed discussions of two specific developments: segmentation into morphemes and the construction of wh questions. Finally we review what we have learned about the role of "training variables" in grammar acquisition.

A Portion of Adam III

The sentence *Where those dogs goed?* was not actually created by Adam in III; it is a composite that illustrates more of the interesting features of his grammar than does any single sentence he actually formed. Let us follow the derivation of this composite sentence using the grammar constructed for Adam at III.

The grammar is a set of mechanical procedures or algorithms for generating sentences and assigning structural descriptions to them. The generation in question is "logical" rather than "psychological," in the sense that the grammar does not constitute a model of practical processes by which sentences might actually be produced or understood. The grammar is psychological in that it is supposed to *represent* Adam's knowledge about the organization of sentences, and it is presumed that this knowledge somehow enters into actual production and comprehension.

30

The structure of grammatical knowledge is not given in any direct and simple way in spontaneous speech. It is worked out from spontaneous speech by a process of inference that is far from being either mechanical or certainly correct. The process is something like trying to fit together the pieces of an immense jigsaw puzzle and something like the process of trying to decipher an unknown Minoan script but not at all like the process of doing experiments in a psychological laboratory. We operate on the general assumption that the child's terminal state of knowledge is of the kind represented by current transformational grammars (e.g., Chomsky, 1965; Katz & Postal, 1964; Klima, 1964). However, we do not simply attribute to each sentence that the child produces the analysis that would be appropriate to that sentence if it were produced by an adult; if we were to do that, the inquiry would be largely vacuous. Insofar as the child's particular sentence — and all related sentences — depart from adult forms, the grammar is tailored to the departures. The most informative departures are analogical errors of commission, such as *goed* in the sample sentence. Harder to interpret, but still important, are errors of omission, such as the absence of the auxiliary *did* from the sample sentence. Omissions in a sentence are at least easy to detect, but omissions in the distributional range of a form are harder to detect and harder to interpret since it is necessary to weigh the probability that an omission is simply a consequence of the size of the sample that has been taken. Finally, all the errors that occur must be considered in comparison with conceivable errors that do not occur. Even this full procedure will not render the construction completely determinate in all respects. The indeterminacies are tentatively resolved by assigning the usual adult representation insofar as that representation does not depend on forms that have never appeared in the child's speech. We shall be able to illustrate most aspects of this process in what follows.

THE PHRASE STRUCTURE LEVEL

A phrase structure rule in adult grammar rewrites a single symbol into symbol(s) distinct from the one rewritten. Roughly speaking, the phrase structure represents the adult's sense of hierarchical grouping in a sentence — the feeling that a sentence cracks or breaks up into natural major constituents which in turn break up into natural smaller constituents. It also represents such basic sentence relations as are called in traditional grammar subject of a sentence, predicate of a sentence, object of a verb, and so forth. The phrase structure includes everything essential for a complete semantic interpretation, but it does not necessarily order elements as they are ordered in the ultimate surface structure.

In the list of phrase structure rules and derivation below each derivation begins with the symbol S for *sentence*, not because Adam is supposed to have a generic intention to compose a sentence which precedes the composition of any particular sentence, but because the grammar is a kind of extended definition of the meaning of *sentence*. The first rule of the phrase

List of Phrase Structure Rules and Derivation

Rules of Phrase Structure	Derivation of "Where those dogs goed?"
1. S → ([imp/wh]) (neg) Nominal–Predicate	wh–Nominal–Predicate
2. Predicate → [MV/Cop]	wh–Nominal–MV
3. MV → Vb (Comp)	wh–Nominal–Vb–Comp
4. Vb → (Aux) V (Prt)	wh–Nominal–Aux–V–Comp
5. Aux → [Vᵉ/B+ing/Past]	wh–Nominal–Past–V–Comp
6. Comp → [Adverb/Nominal (Adverb)]	wh–Nominal–Past–V–Adverb
7. Cop → B–Pred	
8. B → [be/β]	
9. Pred → [Det/Nominal/Adverb]	
10. Adverb → [Loc/Adv/Prep Phr]	wh–Nominal–Past–V–Loc
11. Loc → [somewhere/Adv/Prep Phr]..	wh–Nominal–Past–V–somewhere
12. Prep Phr → Prp[Nominal/Adv]	
13. Nominal → [something/NP]	wh–NP–Past–V–somewhere
14. NP → (Det) N	wh–Det–N–Past–V–somewhere

KEY

Symbols do not all have exact equivalents in the terminology of traditional grammar so translations are only suggestive. The exact sense of each symbol is given by the grammar itself.

( ): optionality
[x/y]: mutual exclusivity of
  x and y
Adv: adverb
Adverb: adverbial
Aux: auxiliary
B: *be* or β
B+ing: progressive aspect
β: should contain *be* form but
  does not
Comp: complement
Cop: copula
Det: determiner or descriptive
  adjective
imp: imperative
Loc: locative adverbial

MV: main verb
N: noun
neg: negative
NP: noun phrase
Past: past tense
Pred: predicate adjectival,
  nominal, or adverbial
Prp: preposition
Prep Phr: prepositional
  phrase
Prt: particle
S: sentence
Vᵉ: catenative verb
V: verb
Vb: verbal
wh: interrogative

structure rewrites S into Nominal and Predicate and a set of abstract morphemes symbolized as imp, wh, and neg. These last three represent the germs from which, respectively, imperatives, interrogatives, and negatives can be developed. The abstract morphemes do not stand for any particular words but provide the occasion in adult grammar for transformations that result in a great variety of imperative, interrogative, and negative expressions. The abstract morphemes are in parentheses; sentences need not be either imperative, interrogative, or negative. In the derivation of a declarative affirmative sentence none of the abstract morphemes is selected. The imp and wh symbols are in brackets to indicate that the symbols are mutually exclusive; a sentence is not simultaneously imperative and interrogative.

The second rule of the phrase structure makes a fundamental division among predicates. The symbol Cop (for *copula*) expands either as a form of *be* or as β, which ultimately has no phonological representation (Adam produces sentences such as *That my book* which should contain a *be* form but do not). Sentences with Cop are sometimes called equational sentences. The verb (or its absence) is followed in such sentences by a noun phrase (NP) functioning as predicate nominative or an adverbial (Adverb) or a descriptive adjective (included in Det which means *determiner*). Sample sentences are *That's a clock, Doggie is here, Doggie big*. The main verb (MV) form of the predicate may, if the verb is a transitive, be followed by a NP functioning as direct object which may in turn be followed by some sort of adverbial (Adverb). Intransitive verbs take adverbials but not direct objects.

In Rule 4 the auxiliary (Aux) is introduced and in Rule 5 it is rewritten. These rules are somewhat different from the rules that represent adult use of the adult auxiliary. What kinds of distributional facts about Adam's speech suggest the rules we have written? Adam's Aux is introduced into MV but not Cop; the adult auxiliary would be introduced into both. The adult rule represents the fact that adults combine *be* forms with Past (e.g., *was*) and with auxiliary verbs (e.g., *I want to be*) and with progressive (B+ing) aspect (e.g., *He is being good*) as well as combining main verbs with these operations. Adam, on the other hand, never combined *be* with auxiliary operations. The division between equational and main verb sentences lies deep in Adam's grammar precisely because he includes Aux in the one and not the other.

In Rule 5 Aux is rewritten as three constituents: catenative verbs (V^c)

such as *wanna, gonna,* and *hafta*; the progressive aspect (B+ing) which produces such forms as *walking* and *eating*; the Past morpheme which produces such forms as *walked* and also *feeled*. Why are the three constituents collected together and placed before the V? The description is not in accord with the surface characteristics of Adam's relevant sentences, for, although the catenatives do precede verbs on the surface, the progressive and past inflections are affixed to the ends of verbs. At a later point in the grammar, in the transformational component, there has to be a rule that transposes stems and affixes so as to produce the correct surface order. In that case why set them wrong in the first place? For several reasons. In the first place, as a means of representing the relation of mutual exclusion which obtains among the three auxiliary elements in Adam's speech. He never combines two or more auxiliaries to say such things as *I was eating* or *I wanted to eat*, though adults of course do. Deeper motivation for the Aux constituent derives from the requirements of the transformational component. In the construction of imperatives, for example, Adam never uses an auxiliary. He says *Please read* but not *Please reading* or *Please wanna read* or *Please readed*. It is convenient to be able to exclude all of the possibilities at once by forbidding the use of all auxiliaries in imperatives and for that you need an Aux constituent. Behind the convenience, of course, is the fact that catenative verbs, progressives, and pasts are distributed in sentences as if they were, on some level, one thing.

These are some of the considerations that shape the first five rules. How does one use the rules to construct a derivation? The derivation of a sentence is, essentially, the pathway through the rules that will yield the sentence. There must be such a pathway for every sentence and none for nonsentences. One constructs a derivation by applying the rules to successive strings, making those (permitted) choices which will in the end produce the intended sentence. The first step of the derivation in the list on page 32 might be read, "the symbol S is rewritten, by Rule 1, as 'wh-Nominal-Predicate.'" Since the intended sentence is to be an interrogative, wh is chosen from among the optional abstract morphemes. The intended sentence is to contain a main verb (*go*) and so MV is selected by Rule 2. The sentence will also contain a locative, and since these develop out of the complement (Comp), that constituent must be added by Rule 3. There is to be a Past auxiliary, and Rules 4 and 5 accomplish its selection.

And so the derivation proceeds. The last line, sometimes called the "preterminal" string, still does not look much like the sentence *Where those dogs goed?* Instead of the interrogative word *where*, we have the abstract interrogative morpheme wh and the locative "somewhere." This last is not the word *somewhere* but rather is a dummy element standing for an unknown, or unspecified, locative. The *where* interrogative will be derived by transformation from the wh element and the dummy locative. The preterminal string contains, in place of the lexical items *those*, *dog*, and *go*, symbols for the categories (or parts of speech) to which these items respectively belong: Det, N, and V. In the next level of the grammar the category symbols will be replaced by appropriate lexical items, and the result will be a terminal string: "wh–those–dog–Past–go–somewhere."

THE SUBCATEGORIZATION LEVEL

If determiners, nouns, and verbs from the lexicon were allowed freely to replace the category symbols Det, N, and V in the preterminal string underlying the sample sentence, the results would often be ungrammatical. In addition to *those dogs go*, we might have *a dogs go, those Adam go, the stone knows*, and what not. There are, in English, restrictions on the co-occurrence of lexical items forbidding many of the combinations that the phrase structure rules alone permit. These restrictions have traditionally been formulated in terms of lexical subcategories. For example, among nouns, those that may take determiners are said to belong to the subcategory of common noun, such as *dog*. Nouns that may not take determiners are proper nouns, such as *Adam*. Nouns are also subcategorized on other principles; count nouns (including *dog*) may be pluralized, whereas mass nouns (e.g., *air*) may not. How is subcategorization to be represented in the present grammar? We shall illustrate the general character of the rules with reference to one constituent of the sample sentence, the subject Nominal, which is represented in the preterminal string as Det-N and in the surface sentence as *those dogs*.

Each entry in the lexicon of the language is going to be assigned certain syntactic features (such as +ct for count nouns) that represent certain distributional potentialities of the lexical items. In addition, the lexical category symbols in the last line of the phrase structure derivation — such as Det, N, and V — are going to expand into complex symbols that also contain syntactic features. The complete complex symbol will be a kind of grappling hook with a set of syntactic features constituting a denticulate surface shaped to retrieve only the right kind of item from the lexicon.

The complex symbol is, first of all, marked with the name of the major

List of Subcategorization Rules and Derivation

Subcategorization Rules		
LEXICAL CATEGORY	CATEGORICAL CONTEXTS	OTHER SYNTACTIC FEATURES
N → [+N][a]	N → [+Det__]; [−Det__]	N → [+ct]; [−ct]
		N → [+no]; [−no]
Det → [+Det][b]		Det → [__[+ct]N]; [__[−ct]N]
		Det → [__[+no]N]; [__[−no]N]

Derivation	
Preterminal string	wh–Det–N–Past–V–somewhere
Complex symbol expansion	N → [+N, +Det__, +ct, +no]
	Det → [+Det, __[+ct]N, __[+no]N]
Replacement by lexical items . .	*dog*, [+N, +Det__, +ct, +no]
	those, [+Det, __[+ct]N, __[+no]N]

[a] Lexical entry: *dog*, [+N, +Det__, +ct, ±no]
[b] Lexical entry: *those*, [+Det, __[+ct]N, __[+no]N]

category (e.g., +N). In the lexicon all nouns (e.g., *dog* in the subcategorization rules and derivation, above) are assumed to be similarly marked. Now we have the first level of subcategorization, sometimes called strict subcategorization. This involves the assignment to each complex symbol of syntactic features which are simply its frames or contexts stated in category symbols. It is as if one were to scan the preterminal string, to take note of the fact that each category occurs in the context of certain other categories, and then to enter those category contexts which restrict the selection of lexical items. In our own example the symbol N occurs in the context Det__. When, therefore, N is replaced by a particular noun from the lexicon, that noun must be of the kind that may be preceded by a determiner — in fact, by a common and not by a proper noun. The facts can be expressed by assigning the complex symbol for N the contextual feature [+Det__], by assigning all common nouns in the lexicon (including *dog*) this same feature, and by adopting a replacement rule which allows the complex symbol for N to be replaced by only those lexical items with matching syntactic features.

From Rule 14 of the phrase structure we know that *in general*, which means across all sentences, determiners are optional before nouns. In the particular sentence under derivation, however, there is to be a determiner before the noun, and that fact must enter into the derivation. The need for specification of a contextual feature arises only, but always, where there is in the phrase structure an optional environment for a lexical category.

Contextual features are needed at several points in Adam's grammar. By assigning verbs the contextual features +__NP and −__NP, for instance, it is possible to retrieve transitive verbs when they are required and intransitives when they are required.

At the next level in the expansion of the complex symbol, syntactic features are added which are not defined in terms of the categories of the preterminal string. In the case of the nouns in a sentence the syntactic features are context-free — that is, they are selected without reference to other complex symbols in the sentence. The syntactic features added to the symbols for determiners and verbs are context-sensitive — they are selected with reference to markers already added to nouns. Such rules are sometimes called selection rules. By this arrangement other words are made to agree with nouns rather than nouns with them. For English, in general, and also for Adam III, the selectional dominance of the noun is not just a convention, but it is rather a representation of certain facts about sentences.

The symbol N in our present derivation acquires the marker +ct rather than −ct and the marker +no rather than −no. It is then equipped to retrieve a count noun from the lexicon, a noun marked +ct as *dog* is on page 36. Lexical entries for nouns will not be marked +no but rather ±no, to indicate that they may be pluralized, or else −no, to indicate that, like *air*, they may not be pluralized. These markers, and in addition a marker that indicates whether a noun is human (+hum) or not, are needed for nouns in Adam III.

The symbol Det acquires syntactic features in a context-sensitive manner, taking its lead, as it were, from the head word in the noun phrase. Since that head word, the N, has the features +ct and +no, the determiner to accompany it must have features which comprise a matrix to the noun's patrix. Det requires the features [__[+ct] N] and [__[+no] N]; the features require that the determiner drawn from the lexicon be one able to modify count nouns in the plural.

The fully expanded complex symbols for our sentence (there would be one for V as well as N and Det) serve to select lexical entries. The general lexical rule (which need not be stated in the formal grammar, since it constitutes part of the definition of derivation) is, Where a complex symbol is not distinct from a lexical entry the latter can replace the former. The lexical entry for *dog* is one of those common count nouns that can replace the symbol for N in the present derivation, and *those* is among the entries that can replace the symbol for Det. These processes are illustrated in the rules and derivation on page 36.

THE TRANSFORMATIONAL LEVEL

The phrase structure and subcategorization levels together comprise what has been called the base structure of a grammar. In a derivation the base structure yields a structured string of morphemes such as wh–[those dog] $_{Nominal}$ [Past–go] $_{Vb}$–somewhere; this string contains only some of its labeled bracketings. Transformational rules map such underlying strings into new structured strings that are closer to actual sentences. Transformations delete, substitute, and permute elements — as phrase structure rules cannot. Roughly speaking, transformations represent the feeling native speakers have that the members of a certain set of sentences are related to their counterparts in another set by a single function.

List of Transformation Rules and Derivation

Transformation Rules[a]

XIV. Wh incorporation for MV sentences:
   wh–Nominal–Vb(Nominal)–somewhere *implies* wh+somewhere–Nominal–Vb (Nominal)
XIX. Affixation of Past[b]:
   χ^1–[Past]$_{Aux}$–V–χ^2 *implies* χ^1–V+Past–χ^2

Derivation

Base: wh–[those dog]$_{Nominal}$[Past–go]$_{Vb}$–somewhere
XIV: wh+somewhere–those–dog–Past–go
XIX: wh+somewhere–those–dog–go+Past

---

[a] The numbers assigned the rules are those they carry in the full grammar.
[b] χ^1 and χ^2 simply stand for any other sentence constituents.

Adam III includes twenty-four transformational rules. Some of the grammatical functions they perform are: agreement in person and number for subject and verb; agreement in number for subject and predicate nominative; creation of such elliptical possessives as *yours* and *mines*; and deletion of subject *you* from imperatives. In the derivation of our sample sentence, transformations are needed to transpose an affix and stem and to incorporate *somewhere* into wh. The rules and the steps in the derivation appear in the list above. A transformational rule describes the structure of the kind of string to which it is applicable; there will generally be an indefinite number of strings that satisfy that structural description. In an actual derivation it is a particular string that is transformed.

THE MORPHOPHONEMIC LEVEL

Rules on this level really belong to the phonological component, but to bring the derivation of our composite sentence to a recognizable form we need to use two of them. They are: xv, wh+somewhere $\rightarrow$ *where*, and xxiv, $[\chi]_V$+Past $\rightarrow \chi$+−*ed*. Rule xxiv results in the erroneous form *goed*. The occurrence of this error marks the absence from Adam III of the adult morphophonemic rule, $[go]_V$+Past $\rightarrow$ *went*. In terms of the conventions with which we are working, then, the error in question is a superficial one. It can be corrected by adding a single rule which does not disturb the remainder of the grammar in any way.

Now that we have a general picture of the children's competence at III, let us characterize in a general way developments between I and III.

Overview of Developments between I and III

Figure 1 indicates that there are large differences in rate of linguistic development among Adam, Eve, and Sarah but the order of events is, for these three unacquainted children, strikingly uniform. So much so that it is possible to describe developments between I and III in a way that is true of all. This is not to say that there are no differences among the children. One that is especially consistent and interesting concerns the rate of production of ungrammatical and anomalous forms. Adam produced these at about four times the rate of either girl—he spoke of "talking crackers," said his nose could "see," addressed the microphone as if it were a person, and said, "It's went," "Why I can't do that," and "That a my book." The girls were more literal and, except for telegraphic omissions, more often grammatical. From other data we have seen and from what parents tell us, there is evidently great individual variation among children on this dimension; probably it explains the very different notions of language development that particular psychologists derive from their own children. When the girls made errors, they were the same kinds of errors that Adam made. For that reason we have assumed that the induction and hypothesis-testing involved is common to the three and simply more copiously externalized by Adam. He gives us a richer print-out, and so we more often cite evidence from his records than from the girls'.

TYPES OF SENTENCES

From I to III the children seem to be working chiefly on simple sentences. This is not to say that all or even most of the children's *utterances* were complete simple sentences. It is rather to say that the most complex construuctions they produced were simple sentences, that they never (or almost never) conjoined or embedded simple sentences. We do not find such sentences as *John and Mary laughed, The man you saw is here*, or *I want you to eat.*

In saying that the children from I to III seemed to be working on the structure of simple sentences it is necessary to make explicit the fact that we do not intend to make two related but stronger claims: We do not claim that in I and III the children learned nothing about conjoining and embedding; it is possible, after all, that some restriction on performance prevented them from revealing in spontaneous speech all that they had learned. Nor do we say that the children's knowledge of the simple sentence was complete before they started to embed and conjoin; that is clearly untrue. In III there were a few instances of embedding, and at that point all three children still had a great deal to learn about simple sentences. Auxiliary elements were only occurring singly; there were no combinations. There were no passives and only the simplest reflexes of negativity. There were no tag questions, and indeed, well-formed yes-no questions of all kinds were missing. Clearly, embedding and conjoining do not wait upon the development of complete knowledge of simple sentences.

What sorts of simple sentences were the children working on from I to III? Declarative-affirmative sentences, of course, but we shall leave till last the description of these, since most of the knowledge involved is not specific to them but is common to all sentences. In addition to declarative-affirmative sentences, the children were working on negatives, imperatives, and interrogatives. We saw in Adam III that these are developed, in transformational grammar, from the abstract morphemes neg, imp, and wh. From the beginning of our records, that is, from I, the children gave evidence of understanding the meaning of these morphemes. What they lacked was the transformational rules which develop surface structures expressing these morphemes. These rules were missing entirely in I. In III there were eight to twelve transformational rules serving this purpose, only a fraction of the adult rules, and some of them were not proper adult rules at all.

René Spitz (1957) says that the child begins at about fifteen months to shake his head as an intentional negative signal, usually having the sense of resistance to some attempt to influence him. In I, we find this signal and also the word *no* used to resist imperatives and to answer yes-no questions.

We also find *no* added initially to several kinds of utterance: *No fall, No put, No picture in there*, and so forth; this seems to be the child's own invention. In II and III the *no* forms were supplemented by *can't, won't*, and *don't*. It seems unlikely to us that these were related transformationally, as they are in the adult language, to *can, will*, and *do* — unlikely because the affirmative modal auxiliaries had not appeared at this time. The forms seemed simply to be a set of preverbal forms introduced by obligatory transformation when the neg morpheme was in the base structure of a sentence with a main verb.

Imperative sentences in adult grammar are derived by transformation out of underlying strings containing the morpheme imp and having *you* as subject and *will* as auxiliary. This analysis is motivated by such adult sentences as, *Go chase yourself* and *Come here, will you?* Neither reflexives (*yourself*) nor tags (*will you*) occurred in early child speech, and so the facts justifying the adult analysis were lacking. In the recording sessions at home one could often be quite sure that a child's sentence had an imperative meaning, but there was nothing in the surface form of his imperative sentences that could serve as a reliable sign of this meaning. To be sure, such sentences were often produced without explicit subject, as are adult imperatives, but the children also very often omitted the subjects of sentences clearly intended to be declaratives. What happened between I and III was that the subjectless sentence came to be ever more nearly restricted to the imperative, but it was not exclusively imperative even in III. In addition, there were a few words the child learned to use after I (especially *please* and *gimme*) which may be confidently interpreted as imperative markers.

Very few of the linguistic reflexes of imperativity developed, then, in this first period, but from the start in I there were indications that the child understood the imperative meaning. This evidence on the responsive side lay in the child's compliance with or (at least as often) resistance to the force of a parental imperative. On the performance side the evidence lay in the child's occasional persistence in using certain constructions again and again to accomplish some effect in a resistant adult.

Interrogatives are of two basic types: yes-no questions and wh questions. We shall leave for a later section the description of wh questions. From I to III the child's yes-no questions were identifiable by rising intonation but not, consistently, by any other feature. It was as if he asked, "Yes or no?" by speaking any sentence or sentence fragment with questioning intonation. Well-formed yes-no questions, with the subject and the first member of the auxiliary transposed, appeared later than III.

The grammatical structure of declarative affirmative simple sentences is represented almost entirely by the base component of a grammar, the phrase structure and subcategorization rules. All of this structure is relevant also to negatives, imperatives, and interrogatives, but these three kinds of sentence include something more — rules in the transformational component. There are several kinds of knowledge represented by the base component: relations within a sentence, a hierarchy of constituents, and subcategorization or co-occurrence restrictions. We shall say something about each of them.

BASIC SENTENCE RELATIONS

The basic relations are those called subject of the sentence, predicate of the sentence, and object of the verb. So far as our materials permit us to judge, the child's knowledge of these relations (which, in English, are chiefly expressed by order) undergoes no development. He seems to express the relations he means to express from the very start. At any rate, there are few detectable errors in all the records. In most utterances it is clear that the intended subject and object are the constituents found in subject and object position — for instance, *I dump trash out, I making coffee, You need some paper*. It is unlikely that the child intended to convey the reversed relations, *Trash dump me out, Coffee making me, Some paper need you*. There are in the records a handful of exceptions in which the intended object seems to be in subject position — *Paper find, Daddy suitcase go get it, Paper write* — but these are the only exceptions in thousands of well-ordered sentences.

The precision with which the child expresses basic sentence relations is important, since these relations are probably linguistic universals and so may themselves be organizations preformed in the human brain. Perhaps subject and object relations are to the child what nut-burying is to the squirrel, an innate pattern requiring only a releaser to set it in operation. Perhaps, but we shall not want to draw that conclusion until we have more data. The children we have studied scrupulously preserve sentence word order not only with respect to basic relations but also with respect to the order of articles, adjectives, auxiliary verbs, adverbs, and all other words. In imitation tasks they omit words but seldom confuse order. This may be a general feature of imitation in children or perhaps only a feature of the imitation of speech. The accurate expression of sentence relations by children learning English may, therefore, be a kind of incidental consequence of the fact that English expresses these relations by word order. We should like to know how well the relations are expressed by children learning a language that expresses subject and object relations by case endings (see Slobin, 1966, for some evidence concerning Russian).

The Aux is a constituent that developed in the period I–III. In I, all main verbs occurred in unmarked generic form. In II and III, the same set of operations on the verb developed in all three children: the progressive, the past, and a set of semi-auxiliary verbs we called catenatives. Most prominent among the catenatives are *gonna*, *wanna*, and *hafta*. The three operations on the verb are represented as a constituent Aux for reasons already described.

The constituent NP was present even in I but underwent consolidation and elaboration between I and III. The constituent status of the NP even in I is attested to by the fact that the children quite consistently responded to questions in *Who* or *What* with some sort of NP. This equivalence in the exchanges of discourse is evidence that the many particular NP's were organized together. In adult speech, the NP has four principal functions in simple sentences: in equational sentences it serves as subject and as predicate nominative, and in main verb sentences as subject and direct object. For the children, the NP had these four functions from the start. At any rate some sort of NP served each function, but, whereas an adult will use every sort of NP in all positions, in the children's speech at I, each position seemed to require a somewhat different formula for the NP. Subjects of equational sentences were often impersonal pronouns (especially *that* and *it*), but predicate nominatives never were. Subjects of main verbs were almost always names of persons or animals, whereas direct objects were almost always names of inanimate things. Subject NP's in both kinds of sentence, at I, never consisted of more than one morpheme — a simple pronoun or noun. Object and predicate nominative NP's at I were, on the other hand, somewhat more complex; they might consist of two nouns (e.g., *Adam book*) or a determiner and noun (e.g., *my book*). If we write a grammar that stays close to the sentences actually obtained at I, we must include four distinct versions of NP, which makes a fragmentary grammar strangely unlike the adult form. One of the things that happened between

43

I and III was that the four NP's came to resemble one another closely enough so that a single NP symbol, one rewritten by a single set of rules, could be entered in all four positions. In addition, the NP grew in complexity in all positions.

There are, finally, constituents that had still not developed by III. These include the adverbials Time and Manner. There were occasional time and manner expressions in the children's speech by III, but they were few. Most importantly, the children at III were not giving grammatically appropriate answers to time (*When*) and manner (*How*) questions. Of the adverbials, the locative is by far the first to develop. It is clearly present even in I.

The progressive inflection (*-ing*) emerged for all three children between I and III. In adult English, this inflection is not used with all verbs. So-called "process" verbs (*sing, walk, eat*, and so forth) freely take the progressive, whereas "state" verbs (*need, equal, know*, and *like*) do not. To say *I am singing the song* is quite correct, but *I am knowing the song* is strange. The process-state subcategorization of verbs can be represented, in an English grammar, in the expansion of the complex symbol for V. A choice is made between two features which represent contexts at the level of the phrase structure, the features $[+[be+ing]\_\_]$; $[-[be+ing]\_\_]$.* These features are entered also in relevant verbs in the lexicon. The interesting fact is that these rules were already needed for the children's grammar at III because the children observed the subcategories and made no mistakes of the type *I liking candy* or *I wanting a book*. Such mistakes were not absent simply from the samples used for the grammars; they were absent from all data over the full range I–V.

David McNeill (1966) has argued that children must have innate knowledge of a hierarchy of subcategories corresponding to whatever hierarchy may prove to be a linguistic universal. The complete absence of subcategorization errors in connection with the progressive inflection seems to support McNeill's position — or, at any rate, does so if the following interpretation of his position is acceptable.

If we ask what could possibly be universal and therefore innate about the process-state distinction, the answer must surely be the underlying

---

* The form be+ing refers to English grammar, whereas the form used earlier, B+ing, refers specifically to the grammar of the children in this study.

semantic principle. The distributional facts, such as the rule for -ing, are known to be specific to particular languages. How could an innate process-state distinction forestall inflectional errors? Something like this would have to be true: As the meaning was learned of each new verb like *walk*, *eat*, *need*, and *like*, the semantic entry would have to include all innate subcategorization features as well as individual elements of meaning. In short, *walk* would from the first be tagged as a "process" and *need* as a "state."

When at a later time the child attended to distributional facts peculiar to English, such as the fact that some verbs are inflected with -ing and some not, he would have a set of ready hypotheses to explain the cleavage. He would test to see whether it was governed by one or another of the pre-established, universal subcategorizations. And of course the process-state subcategorization defines the proper dotted line for -ing. It is somewhat as if a child learning to recognize coins kept track of all the attributes that are ever significant in a coinage system — color, weight, size, design, texture, and so forth. Then when he first encountered the distributional facts of monetary exchange, such as the fact that two coins of one kind equal one of another, he would quickly see which of the perceptual attributes he had been keeping track of were useful.

The absence of error in connection with a semantically principled subcategorization is one prediction of the "innateness" hypothesis, and this prediction is confirmed in the case of the progressive. However, one easily thinks of other predictions that are not confirmed. The division of nouns into mass and count subcategories is semantically based and as likely to be universal as the process-state division, but the children were, at V, still making some errors in their use of the noun subcategories. Some subcategorizations in English are unprincipled (i.e., they have no semantic base) — for example, the verb subcategories that take regular and irregular inflections for Past. Not surprisingly, children make many mistakes in cases like these, where rote learning of the subcategory membership of each verb is really the only possibility. In fact, errors in this connection are often heard in the elementary school years; they are to be expected. But if the children have innate subcategories, should they not, on first encountering unprincipled cleavages, act as if they expected one or another of the innate principles to govern the cleavage? On first encountering the fact that some verbs take -ed and some do not, a child ought to test the hypothesis that all of the former verbs might be processes and the latter states, the hypothesis that the former might be transitives and the latter intransitives, and so forth. There is no trace of anything of the kind in our data.

The full story is too long to tell, but our present best guess is that the absence of error with *-ing* is not to be attributed to innate subcategorization. And, in general, we have not found any reason to believe that subcategories are innate other than the usual reason — it is exceedingly difficult to determine how they are learned.

NONCATEGORICAL SYNTACTIC FEATURES

Plural number in English is marked by inflection of the noun; this inflection, like the progressive, was entirely absent in I and often present by III. The expression of number in English is vastly more complicated than the expression of something like progressive aspect. For example, there must be agreement in number between a head noun and its determiners, between a subject noun and a predicate nominal, and between a pronoun and its antecedent noun. Number and person together, as features of a subject noun, determine the form of the verb: *walks* or *walk*, *is* or *are*. In Adam III, number is introduced in the base structure in the form of two context-free syntactic markers in the complex symbol for the noun: [+no] and [−no]. There are related markers for the complex symbol of Det and for many lexical items. There are three transformations and several morphophonemic rules.

The development of number in the three children illustrates nicely the difference between deep and superficial acquisition of a grammatical feature. In terms of chronological age, Eve began to inflect nouns some fourteen months earlier than did Sarah. However, when Eve first used plurals she made many mistakes in all aspects of number agreement, whereas Sarah, from the start, made almost no mistakes. What this means is that in Eve's grammar, number first appears as a low-level morphophonemic rule which, in effect, says that nouns have an optional pronunciation with a terminal sibilant. The introduction of this rule leaves the rest of Eve's grammar undisturbed. For Sarah, number enters in the base structure and effects complex changes in the total grammar. So we see that Eve was not always so far in advance of Sarah as the simple mean length of utterance index alone would indicate. And we see that acquisitions that may look alike if only certain words or endings are examined may look very unlike when the total distributional pattern is examined.

46

In summary of this overview, it is correct to say that the child's early grammar comprises a base structure not very different from that of the adult grammar and a syntactic transformational component that is rudimentary in III and almost totally absent in I. This is not the same as saying that children directly speak base-structure sentences. It is not clear what that statement could mean since morphophonemic and phonetic rules are required to make sentences of the underlying strings. But the underlying strings themselves seem to be chiefly those that can be generated by the base.

Segmentation into Morphemes

In order to learn grammar, a child must segment the speech he hears into morphemes because morphemes are the ultimate units of grammatical rules. There are short-run regularities that can be formulated in smaller units, the segmental phonemes, but the long-run regularities that render an infinite number of meanings constructable and interpretable cannot be formulated in terms of phonemes.

It may be useful to imagine an erroneous segmentation into morphemes and what its consequences would be. Consider the following set of utterances that a child might easily hear: *My book, Your book; My bike, Your bike; My birthday, Your birthday*. If we let a slash mark represent a morpheme cut, then this segmentation is erroneous; *Myb/ook, Yourb/ook; Myb/ike, Yourb/ike; Myb/irthday, Yourb/irthday*. These morphemes look odd in print, but they represent sound combinations that are, in English phonology, easily pronounceable — think of *scribe* and *orb*, *Ike* and *oops*.

Suppose the child who has segmented in the above fashion goes on to store the contexts of each morpheme to the (unintentional and unconscious) end of discovering general and meaningful construction rules. The result may be represented in part as:

$$myb, [\_\_ook, \_\_ike, \_\_irthday]$$
$$yourb, [\_\_ook, \_\_ike, \_\_irthday]$$
$$ook, [myb\_\_, yourb\_\_]$$
$$ike, [myb\_\_, yourb\_\_]$$

Myb and *yourb* have identical context entries distinct from the entries for *ook* and *ike*, the latter two being themselves identical. In these circumstances it would be reasonable to infer the existence of two morpheme classes ($C_1 \rightarrow myb, yourb$; $C_2 \rightarrow ook, ike, irthday$) and of a construction signifying possession which is created by selecting class members in proper sequence (C_1–C_2). These inferences founded on a mistaken segmentation do not lead anywhere. For the small set of utterances that preserve the artificial co-occurrence of certain morphemes and a subsequent /b/ phoneme, the segmentation would appear to work. Given *my b/rake* and *my b/and*, the child could construct *your b/rake* and *your b/and* with approximately correct meaning. However, outside this artificial range his false morphemes would not work. He would not hear *the ook, the ike, the irthday* or *myb pencil, myb doggie, yourb Mommy*. And he would find unanalyzable such new possessives as *my pencil, my doggie, my Mommy, your pencil*, and *your doggie*.

Compare the results of a correct segmentation. The context entries would look like this:

> *my,* [___ *book,* ___ *bike,* ___ *birthday*]
> *your,* [___ *book,* ___ *bike,* ___ *birthday*]
> *book,* [*my* ___, *your* ___]
> *bike,* [*my* ___, *your* ___]

One morpheme class would represent a start on possessive pronouns, and the other a start on count nouns. A construction rule written in terms of these classes correctly anticipates *your brake* from the occurrence of *my brake, my band* from *your band*, and so on in an indefinite number of cases. Furthermore, the tentative morphemes *book, bike, birthday, my,* and *your* will recur with approximately the same meaning in such new constructions as *the book, my old hat,* and *your good friend*. A correct segmentation is repeatedly confirmed by its continuing ability to unlock regularities and structural meanings. An erroneous segmentation is a false trail winding off into the desert.

Judging from our materials, and from what we know of the materials of others, morpheme segmentation errors such as *myb pencil* or *the ook* are uncommon. It is easy to overlook the segmentation problem in child speech because there is so little evidence that it exists. The evidence we found in the fine structure of our data suggests that segmentation is a real problem in the sense that it is something a child learns but that it is also a problem for which he has highly effective solution procedures.

For example, Adam produced in an early record the sentence *It's big*. What was the status in Adam's grammar of the form *'s* (or *is*)? In adult grammar, *is* is a morpheme distinct from such other morphemes as *it* and *big* and organized closely with *am* and *are* as forms (allomorphs) of the verb *be*. We find in Adam's records certain errors of commission suggesting that *is* was differently organized for him. He produced hundreds of well-formed equational sentences with *it* as subject, but he also produced a large number of odd ones. The following are representative: *It's fell* (Sample 14), *It's has wheels* (Sample 21), *It's hurts* (Sample 17), and *It's went on the top* (Sample 22). The form *is* has no place in these sentences and seems to have been imported into them as an onhanger of *it*. Perhaps, then, the adult polymorphic form *its* was a single unanalyzed morpheme for Adam. How does this hypothesis fare when tested against all the relevant evidence?

Suppose the hypothesis were wrong, and Adam was, in fact, learning to organize *is* in the correct, adult way. What errors ought he then to have made? Since *is*, as a form of *be*, is closely related to *am* and *are*, we should expect the several forms to have occasionally displaced one another in Adam's sentences through disregard of the features of the subject noun phrase that are supposed to select them. There ought to have been such errors as *I is, we is, I are,* and *he am.* There were no such errors in Adam's early records, and that fact supports the conclusion that *is* was not at first organized as a form of *be*.

In certain contexts *is* is obligatory: in such reduced equational sentences as *it big*, and in sentences with a verb inflected for progressive aspect, such as *it going*. When Adam began sometimes to produce an audible *is* in such contexts, he did not, for many months, always do so. On the same page of a protocol, it is quite usual to find otherwise identical sentences with and without *is*. Of course, adults too do not always sound all their segmental phonemes, but this particular reduction, from *it's* to *it*, is not one that adults make. Its occurrence in Adam suggests that for him *it's* and *it* were just varying pronunciations of one morpheme.

The range of *is* in Adam's early records was restricted in an important way. The word *it* is an impersonal pronoun and substitutes for impersonal noun phrases. When such noun phrases themselves occur as subjects of equational sentences and with verbs inflected for progressive aspect, an adult uses *is* — for example, *The top is big; The top is spinning.* In such cases, during the many months when we believe *it-s* was organized as a single morpheme, Adam always failed to produce *is* — that is what should happen if our hypothesis is correct. If, on the contrary, *is* were a separate morpheme, the difference between its invariable absence with noun phrase subjects and its only occasional absence with *it* as subject would be unaccountable.

There is another revealing restriction of range. If *it's* were simply a variant of *it*, then it ought to have occurred sometimes in all the sentence positions that *it* ever fills. As the third column of Table 1 shows, *it* was an object of a verb more often than it was a subject. An adult would never use *it's* as a pronoun object, but our hypothesis about *it's* predicts such errors for Adam. If *it's* were a simple variant of *it*, he ought to have formed such sentences as *get it's* and *put it's there*. As the third column of Table 1 shows, he never made such errors.

The forms *it* and *it's* were in perfect complementary distribution. This is not a phonologically conditioned complementary distribution of the kind that obtains for the several forms of the regular plural inflection in English. In the phonologically conditioned case the several forms are perfectly predictable, so the variation among them is always redundant, and the descriptive linguist (e.g., Gleason, 1961; Harris, 1942; Hockett, 1947; Nida, 1948) considers the forms to be allomorphs of one morpheme. The complementary distribution that obtains for *it* and *it's* seems to be conditioned by grammatical role (sentence subject versus verb object), and in such cases the linguist does not necessarily conclude that the forms are allomorphs or variant forms.

Many languages use inflectional forms to signal the role of a word in a larger construction. When nouns are involved (the most familiar instance), we speak of cases. Subject and object case (or nominative and accusative) are marked in Sanskrit, Latin, Greek, Finnish, and many other languages

Table 1. The Forms *It* and *It's* in Early Adam Samples

Samples	*It* as Subject, *Is* Required as Verb[a]		*It* as Subject, *Is* Forbidden as Verb[b]		*It* as Object, *Is* Forbidden to Occur[c][d]:
	Is Absent	*Is* Present	*Is* Absent	*Is* Present	*Is* Absent
5–7		1			73
8–10		2	1		106
11–13		4	2		89
14–16	4	6	8	2	94
17–19	3	33	2	10	132
20–22	3	54		18	112

[a] For example, *It's big; It's going.*
[b] For example, *It hurts; It went.*
[c] For example, *Get it; Put it there.*
[d] No sentences with *is* present appeared in the sample.

(Gleason, 1961). In English, nouns are not inflected for case; nominative and accusative forms are distinguished by word order (e.g., *John saw Mary* versus *Mary saw John*). However, Adam used *it* and *it's* as if *'s* or *is* were a nominative case ending. If *it* and *it's* were organized in this way, then *is* was a separate morpheme, and we are incorrect in suggesting that *it's* was a single form, a variant of *it*. The possibility is an interesting one. Since case is a common syntactic device in the languages of the world, it is reasonable to suppose that case should be among the hypotheses about linguistic structure that the human mind would be disposed to entertain and test (Chomsky, 1965; Fodor, 1966). Much of the distributional data available to Adam would seem to have confirmed this hypothesis, and he might reasonably have organized the facts about *it* and *it's* in this way until more data motivated reorganization. However, for various reasons that cannot be detailed here, it is quite clear that Adam's *is* was not functioning as a case ending. The conclusion that best fits all the evidence is that *it* and *it's* were allomorphs of a single morpheme, their occurrence conditioned by grammatical role.

Errors of segmentation were rare in Adam, Eve, and Sarah, but *it's* was not the only case. The clearer instances * include: *I'm, that-a, drop-it, get-it, put-it, want-to, have-to, going-to, another-one, what-that*, and *let-me*. These pairs have two characteristics which, taken together, distinguish them from pairs that were correctly analyzed. The first characteristic is a phonetic one. *It's, wanna, lemme, put-it*, and, indeed, all pairs in the set are regularly run together by adults as if they were in fact single words (Heffner, 1949). This is to say that the morpheme boundary is not in these pairs marked in any way whatever — the pairs all lack the open juncture phoneme ($/+/$) which marks the majority of morpheme boundaries in English. Perhaps, then, children are usually able to avoid segmentation errors because they regularly cut the stream of speech at just those points where $/+/$ occurs. This, however, is not a simple claim.

How are children able to recognize $/+/$? It is not a phonetically sim-

---

* Brown and Bellugi (1964) previously interpreted some portions of the relevant evidence in other ways. For instance, errors like *That a my boot* and *That a your car* were thought to indicate that Adam had adopted a mistaken rule permitting articles to precede every sort of nominal other than pronouns. Such errors as *drop it book* and *get it pencil* suggested that Adam, in learning to substitute pronouns for noun phrases, was making both explicit. In certain points of detail, previously overlooked, the view here that *that-a, drop-it,* and *get-it* were all unanalyzed single morphemes provides a closer fit to the data than do the previous interpretations.

ple feature. To be sure, when detectable pauses occur in a sentence, it is usually at morpheme boundaries; pause is thus considered one of the phonetic manifestations of /+/. The difficulty is that pause is only an intermittent feature. How is /+/ identified more generally?

Consider the pairs *nitrate* and *night-rate*, *slyness* and *minus*, *mark it* and *market*. There need be no actual pause in either member of a pair, but still there is an audible difference in the amount of aspiration on the /t/, in the duration of the vowel /ay/, and in the release of /k/. For each pair there is a phoneme that takes two somewhat different forms. In order to be able to classify the related but different sounds as single phonemes and so to simplify description, the linguist creates the junctural phoneme /+/ and assigns to it the phonetic features distinguishing a pair (Harris, 1951). The phonemic transcriptions will then look like this: /nayt+reyt/, /slay+nɨs/, /mark+ət/, /naytreyt/, /maynɨs/, /markət/. It follows that the phonetic values of /+/ are a disjunctive set and elaborately so. It follows also that /+/ is not itself a segment at all, since aspiration, duration, and the like have no existence apart from particular vowels and consonants. The open juncture, in short, is an invention of linguistic science designed to simplify language description. How could a child possibly learn to recognize /+/ and use it to segment the speech he hears?

The /t/ one hears in *night rate* occurs also at the ends of words (e.g., *night* or *right*) and so can occur terminally in complete utterances, whereas the /t/ of *nitrate* is never terminal. Similarly, the /ay/ of slyness can be terminal (as in *sly* or *die*), but the /ay/ of *minus* cannot. And, in general, that form of a phoneme which is found within utterances at morpheme boundaries is found also in final position in total utterances, but the form found within utterances internal to a morpheme is never final in a total utterance. A child might learn that. He might learn also to give special status to utterance-internal consonants or vowels that assumed the forms they ordinarily assumed in utterance-final position. In fact, he might learn to make morpheme cuts at just these points and to make contextual entries in terms of the resultant units.

When a child first begins to produce polymorphemic utterances, he has for some time been producing single-morpheme utterances. Suppose that he has made independent entries for all of these — both the one-morpheme utterances like *dog* and the polymorphemic utterances like *my dog*; at this point, the polymorphemic utterances might simply have the status for him of longer words. Suppose now that an internal analysis routine is activated which involves retrieving two entries at a time and comparing them, phonemically, from left to right. Suppose, further, that he returns to storage pairs with unlike first phonemes but retains for further analysis pairs that start out identically. Let him then make a tentative morphemic cut at the first point of phonemic divergence in the pair. Let him finally look up the resulting segments to see if there are already independent entries for them — as there usually would be if they were morphemes — and mark as morphemes just those segments having prior entries. If he picked a pair like br/eak and br/ing, he would cut them as indicated, would find no prior entries for any of the segments, and would not mark them as morphemes. However, a pair like *my/dog* and *my/cat* would yield segments with prior entries, and a child who started with this pair might soon discover that cuts yielding morphemes by his original criteria regularly coincided with terminal vowels and consonants (or, one might say, with /+/). Thereafter he could make segmentation cuts wherever terminal phonemes occurred without regard to either identical sequences or prior entries. By this account, the value of /+/ is discovered from its correlation with more primitive criteria. It is possible, however, that the terminal vowels and consonants are themselves the most primitive criterion of morpheme segmentation.

Although errors of segmentation seem only to occur across boundaries unmarked by open juncture in adult speech, it is far from the case that every such unmarked boundary will give rise to an error of segmentation. Adults will run together *Pop's here* as well as *It's here*. But Adam organized *is* as a feature in the pronunciation not of any noun but only of the pronoun *it*. Probably the important factor here is the second characteristic, which helps to define the pairs erroneously organized as single morphemes. Each such pair was characterized by a high transition probability in the speech mothers addressed to their children. After the first member, the second was more frequent by far than any other morpheme. Nouns like *Pop* or *Adam* sometimes appeared as subjects of equational sentences, but they also often appeared as subjects of main verbs — too often, apparently, for Adam to make the mistake of thinking *is* belonged to the nouns. *It*, on the other hand, appeared hundreds of times a day as the subject of equational sentences but seldom, surprisingly seldom, as the subject of any other verb. The high transitions in these pairs have nothing to do with grammar, of course, but are simply accidental statistical features of mother-child interaction. They demonstrate that bias in the language sample to which a child is exposed can, in an extreme case, result in a partly erroneous formulation of the underlying grammar.

It is important to make it perfectly clear that the evidence for segmentation errors is not simply, or even primarily phonetic. We are not relying on the fact that Adam's version of *it's* often sounded like *iss* or that his rendering of *want to* sounded like *wanna*. The important evidence is distributional: the fact that Adam said *It's hurts,* for instance, and that he said *I want to play* but never *I want you to play.* When, at length, the children corrected their few segmentation errors and reconstrued the forms of *be* and articles, the evidence was again distributional and in some cases dramatically clear. In the case of Adam's *a,* for example, the form appeared for nineteen samples in only a restricted portion of its proper range — chiefly with *that* as pronoun subject.* Then, in Samples 20 and 21, the full range quite suddenly filled out, and *a* appeared with noun phrases in isolation, noun phrases functioning as subjects of sentences, noun phrases in locative questions, and so forth. We do not yet know what causes reconstruction of forms at one time rather than another.

Transformations in Wh Questions

Wh questions are those using an interrogative word from the set *who, whom, what, where, when, why,* and *how.* Contemporary generative grammars of English (e.g., Katz and Postal, 1964; Klima, 1964) do not all derive wh questions in just the same way, but they all do use transformational rules to represent the systematic relations between these questions and the declaratives that answer them. Wh questions begin to appear in good quantity and variety at Level III; indeed, the composite sentence derived with rules from Adam III was such a question. The question here is whether there is, in the form of these questions, evidence directly supporting the notion that the child acquires implicit knowledge of the kind represented by the transformational rules of the adult grammar. The brief discussion here is drawn from a full research report (Brown, 1968) which presents the evidence for all wh questions in all the protocols from I through V.

Table 2 sets out some adult questions and answers so as to expose the systematic relations among them. Consider first the two middle columns.

---

* The form appeared also with a few strictly transitive verbs where, as with *that,* it seems to have been a feature of pronunciation. Representative errors are: *have a two minute, get a one.*

Table 2. Systematic Relations among Questions and Answers

Constituents to Be Specified	Normal Questions [a][b]	Occasional Questions [a][c]	Possible Answers[a]
Subject nominal	*Who* will read the book?	*WHO* will read the book?	*John* will read the book.
Object nominal	*What* will John read?	John will read *WHAT?*	John will read *the book.*
Predicate nominal	*What* is that?	That is *WHAT?*	That is *a book.*
Predicate	*What* will John do?	John will *do WHAT?*	John will *read the book.*
Locative adverbial	*Where* will John read?	John will read *WHERE?*	John will read *in the library.*
Time adverbial	*When* will John read?	John will read *WHEN?*	John will read *this evening.*
Manner adverbial	*How* will John read?	John will read *HOW?*	John will read *slowly.*

[a] Wh words and the substitutes for them are italicized.
[b] The derivation of normal questions follows: Base: Wh–John–will–read–something; Preposing and Wh incorporation: Wh+something–John–will–read; Transposition: Wh+something–will–John–read; Morphophonemic: What–will–John–read.
[c] Words with all letters capitalized receive heavy stress and rising intonation.

Each question in "normal" form stands alongside a semantically equivalent, but less frequent "occasional" form, in which the wh word is in final position and is to be spoken with heavy stress and rising intonation. If someone said, "John will read the telephone book," one might respond, "John will read *what?*" — this response is an occasional form. The occasional form for the subject nominal — the first entry — is unlike the others in the column in that the wh word appears initially, its normal position.

The occasional forms (except the subject nominal) are all related to their normal counterparts by the same function. In describing the function let us take the occasional form as the base or starting point. The normal form can be created from the occasional in two steps: The first would move the wh word from final position to initial position; we call this preposing. The second would interchange the subject of the sentence and the auxiliary; we call this transposing. The same two steps will generate all the questions of the second column from their respective counterparts in the first column. Essentially, these two steps are the transformational rules used in adult grammar to derive wh questions. The main difference is that normal questions are not derived from actual occasional questions but from underlying strings that are similar to the occasionals.

Consider now the sentences of the last column, which are examples of well-formed answers to the questions standing opposite them. Question and answer differ in the words that are italicized in each case and only in these words. The italicized words in the answers may be said to stand in place of the italicized wh words — in the *exact* place, the very sentence locus of the wh word, for the occasional questions. The normal questions, we know, shift the place of the wh word. The material italicized in the answer is the material most directly responsive to the question. Indeed it is the only essential part of the answer. "What will John read?" *"The book."* "When will John read?" *"This evening."* In fact, each interrogative word is a kind of algebraic x standing in the place of a particular constituent of the sentence, the constituent identified in the left column of Table 2. The wh word asks for specification of that constituent. It marks the spot where information is to be poured into the sentence, and the form of the wh word — whether *who, what, where,* or *when* — indicates the kind of information required.

A transformational grammar of adult English can represent the systematic relations of Table 2 in the following way. Associated with each of the sentence constituents there is a stand-in element symbolized as "someone," "something," "somewhere," "sometime," and "somehow." The derivation of a wh question begins in the phrase structure with the selection of the interrogative morpheme wh. Then, from the constituent which is to be specified in a well-formed answer, the stand-in element is selected, rather than some particular NP, Loc, or whatever. The phrase structure derivation terminates in an underlying string which is just like the string for the occasional question except that the stand-in element stands where the interrogative words stand in the occasional questions of Table 2. In the derivation of normal questions, a first transformation preposes the stand-in element and incorporates it into wh, and a second transformation transposes the order of the subject NP and the first member of the auxiliary. A morphophonemic rule rewrites the wh + stand-in component as the appropriate interrogative word: wh + something as *what*: wh + someone as *who*; wh + somewhere as *where*, and so forth. The derivation rules and sample strings are represented in the note to Table 2.

PRODUCTION OF A HYPOTHETICAL INTERMEDIATE

The composite sentence derived by Adam III was *Where those dogs goed?* and not *Where did those dogs go?* How is Adam's form related to the derivation of the normal adult form? It is a sentence that would be produced by the rules in the note to Table 2 if the second transformation, the one that transposes subject and auxiliary, were simply omitted, and if the morphophonemic rules followed upon the preposing transformation alone. In short, Adam seems to have given phonetic form to a structure that is generated by the adult grammar as a hypothetical intermediate, a structure not actualized as a question by adults. The composite form is, in this respect, representative of all Adam's wh questions in III and for many months after III. Eve and Sarah both also constructed these pre-

Table 3. The Child's Wh Question as a Hypothetical Intermediate
in Adult Grammar

Occasional Questions[a]	Child's Questions[b]	Normal Questions[c]
WHO will read the book?....	Who will read the book?	Who will read the book?
John will read WHAT?	What John will read?	What will John read?
That is WHAT?	What that is?	What is that?
John will do WHAT?........	What John will do?	What will John do?
John will read WHERE?	Where John will read?	Where will John read?

[a] Words with all letters capitalized receive heavy stress and rising intonation.
[b] Derivable from occasional questions by preposing.
[c] Derivable from occasional questions by preposing and transposing.

posed wh questions, though not in such quantity as did Adam. Table 3 represents the relation between the children's version of various wh questions and the two varieties of well-formed adult questions.

A TRANSFORMATION IN DISCOURSE

The derivation rules loosely described in the note to Table 2 and presented in explicit form in Adam III presuppose the establishment of such major sentence constituents as NP and Loc, since the stand-in elements are associated with these constituents. As seen in the Overview of Developments between I and III (pp. 39–47), there was good evidence of the existence of these constituents from early in the records. The most persuasive evidence was the children's ability to answer *who* and *what* questions with noun phrases and *where* questions with locatives. We also reported in the Overview that adverbials of time and manner did not seem to be organized as constituents in I to III, since the children did not make grammatically appropriate answers to *when* and *how* questions. If the responsive constituents were not organized as such, then *when* and *how* questions could not be derived in the children's grammar by the kinds of rules we have proposed. It is consistent, therefore, to find that Adam in III was still not making *when* and *how* questions.

In another respect, Adam's performance in III seems not to have been consistent with the rules. He produced a large number of *why* and *why not* questions. But in all of the prior sixteen samples he had only once answered a *why* question in a way that could possibly be considered appropriate. In this case, then, we seem to have the construction of the question occurring before there is any evidence on the responsive side that the relevant grammatical organization exists.* We have also, incidentally, a demonstration that, in language development, comprehension need not always precede production.

When we look at Adam's *why* and *why not* questions in their actual discourse setting, we find something unexpected and interesting: they were often closely related to an immediately antecedent declarative from his mother. Table 4 contains a set of mother's declaratives and Adam's *why* responses. Some of the differences between members of these pairs are not peculiar to *why* questions. For instance, the telegraphic reduction process

---

* Adult *why* questions cannot be derived in a way directly parallel to other wh questions. We have not gone into the details because they do not alter the fact that Adam produced such questions when his responses gave no evidence that he could analyze them correctly with respect to either grammar or semantics.

that eliminates *was, -ing,* and *a* from the adult sentence is quite general in child speech. Setting aside such nonspecific differences, Adam's questions are a simple function of his mother's antecedent declaratives: the word *why* is placed in front of the declarative. Table 4 also has a set of questions in *why not,* and these, too, have apparent bases in the mother's speech. Setting aside a few details, what happens is that the words *why not* are added in front of the mother's negative declaratives. In creating these questions, Adam seems to have been operating with a rule very like the preposing transformation.

Table 4. *Why* and *Why Not* Questions from Adam 17–19 with Apparent Bases

Mother's Declaratives	Adam's Questions
Why	
He was playing a little tune	Why he play little tune?
I see a seal	Why you see seal?
You bent that game	Why me bent that game?
Well, because she wanted to	Why she want to?
I think it's resting now	Why it's resting now?
Why Not	
I guess I'm not looking in the right place	Why not you looking right place?
Because you weren't careful	Why not me careful?
I don't see any	Why not you see any?
You can't dance	Why not me can't dance?
You're going to have to buy another one and give it to Ursula because you're breaking that one	Why not me break that one?

Where did Adam's *why* and *why not* transformations come from? Once in a long while, his mother produced a *why* question as a direct follow-up of a declarative and repeated in her *why* question the proposition expressed in the declarative. Probably Adam was attempting to imitate this performance, but his imitation did not come out right. Suppose the antecedent declarative were "He can't dance." Mother would follow this with "Why can't he dance?" Adam's version, on the other hand, would be "Why he can't dance?" Mother not only preposed *why,* she also transposed the subject and auxiliary in the manner of the adult grammar. Adam only preposed. Probably he copied according to his present understanding — as children also do when they pretend to drive a car or read a newspaper. Perhaps his imitation took the form it did because that form was close to the general operation that Adam was using with his other wh questions.

So we do have some evidence that the knowledge represented by transformation rules in the derivation of wh questions was learned by the children. They did not simply start to produce well-formed questions at a given point in time. All three children first produced a simpler form that would result from the application of just one of the two transformations required. And Adam — always the one to make interesting errors — also created *why* questions in circumstances that suggest the application of the same single transformation to declarative bases supplied by his mother.

The Role of Training Variables

Whatever the processes by which children acquire grammar, their primary data come from the speech they hear. Part of our work has consisted of attempts to isolate antecedents in the child's linguistic environment which may affect the rate or quality of the child's development. By antecedents we do not mean global variables like social class, but specific features of parental speech and parent-child interaction.

We have learned something about the effects of two aspects of variation in the speech to which a child is exposed: variation in the frequency with which particular constructions are produced or "modeled," and variation in the frequency with which particular reactions are made to a child's utterances. The reactions we have studied are expansions, occasional forms of wh questions, and expressions of approval and disapproval.

The work has progressed through three phases: first, discovery of relations between parental speech and rate of language development in our three subjects; second, a manipulative experiment with different subjects to test a hypothesis derived from those observations; and third, more detailed analyses of relations within our longitudinal data.

PRELIMINARY OBSERVATION AND AN EXPERIMENT

When we began work several years ago, one of the first things we noticed was the frequency with which parents responded to the young child's telegraphic utterance * by echoing what the child said and filling in the missing functors. If the child said *Eve lunch* or *Throw Daddy,* the parent often responded with the nearest complete sentence appropriate in the particular situation — *Eve is having lunch* or *Throw it to Daddy.* Brown and Bellugi (1964) called such responses expansions, and suggested that they might

---

* We have not in this paper discussed the telegraphic aspect of the child's early sentences, since that was a major topic of such earlier papers as Brown and Fraser (1963) and Brown and Bellugi (1964). In I, II, and III, however, the speech of the three children was extremely telegraphic, as the data on page 29 indicate.

provide optimal data for the acquisition of grammar. It was not their intention to suggest that the child learned grammar by storing the expanded versions of his telegraphic utterances, since he could not in this way learn more than the finite set of sentences he had at some time attempted to produce. Brown and Bellugi recognized that expansions were only data, and that grammatical knowledge was a system of general rules somehow derived from data. They argued, however, that the data provided by expansions were maximally relevant and seemed to be delivered with ideal timing.

At the same time, we have always realized that the relevance and timing of particular forms of interaction may have no importance for the acquisition of grammar. It is quite possible that the adult need do nothing but "model" the language — that is, provide samples of well-formed speech. When evidence is limited to natural observations, it is not possible to separate the effect of expansions from the effect of the amount of well-formed speech that the child hears. The mothers of Adam and Eve responded to the speech of their children with expansions about 30 per cent of the time. Sarah's overall language development was slower, and her mother expanded fewer of Sarah's utterances. But Sarah's mother also talked less to her child in general. In our samples of three parents, expansion rate and general volubility varied together, and their effects on language acquisition could not be teased apart.

A manipulative experiment was designed to separate these two aspects of the child's language environment and to compare their effects (Cazden, 1965). The subjects were twelve Negro children, aged twenty-eight to thirty-eight months. They were all attending a private day-care center in Boston, where thirty children under three and a half years were cared for by one adult. Four matched trios were formed on the basis of the child's chronological age, talkativeness, and initial level of language development as judged by his mean length of utterance during an orientation period. Within each trio the children were randomly assigned to one of three treatment groups: expansion, modeling, or control.

The expansion group received forty minutes per day of intensive and deliberate expansions. The modeling group received exposure to an equal number of well-formed sentences that were not expansions. One of two tutors trained for this research talked with each child in these two groups in an individual play session every school day for three months. The sessions were held in two small rooms normally used only for naps; both were equipped with toys and books selected to stimulate conversation. The play sessions were monitored at regular intervals during the three-month period to ensure the separation of the critical interaction variables. Children in the control group received no treatment, but they were brought into the treatment rooms every few days so that they stayed familiar with the materials and the tutors.

Tape recordings were made of each child's speech at the beginning, middle, and end of the three-month period. The tapes were transcribed by a secretary who was trained by a linguist on our staff and who was ignorant of the treatment assignment of the children. The transcriptions were then coded according to strict rules. The dependent variables were six measures of language development: one was a test of the child's ability to repeat sentences, and five measured aspects of the child's spontaneous speech — mean length of utterance in morphemes, noun phrase index, verb complexity, copula index, and type-of-sentence index (the last four indexes were devised for this research).

Two statistical analyses were used to test the hypothesis that expansions would be the most effective treatment. First, the six dependent variables were considered separately. A two-way analysis of variance (treatment x tutor) was computed for the post-test scores on each measure separately, with the pretest scores on that same measure as a covariance control. Then, in order to compare the children on their overall growth on the six measures considered together, growth was operationally defined as the sum of the child's six gain score ranks, and Friedman's nonparametric two-way analysis of variance was used to test the significance of group differences. In neither analysis was there any evidence that expansions aid the acquisition of grammar. Contrary to our hypothesis, modeling was the most effective treatment.

Before speculating on possible explanations for these results, we need to examine what happens when forms of interaction which naturally co-occur are experimentally separated. Originally, we assumed that modeling without expansion had no positive features of its own, but this turns out not to be the case. If a child says *Dog bark* when a dog is indeed barking, the expanding adult says *Yes, the dog is barking.* The non-expanding adult who desires to maintain a reasonable discourse sequence — as our tutors did — has to contribute a related idea, such as, *Yes, he's mad at the kitty* or *Yes, but he won't bite.* Thus, a treatment which focuses on grammatical structure confines the adult to expanded echoes of the child and limits the ideas to the child's presumed meaning, whereas a treatment that focuses on the idea extends that idea beyond the presumed meaning of the child and introduces more varied words and grammatical elements to express those related ideas. In natural conversation, parents often provide both grammatical expansions and semantic extensions. Our tutors were asked not to do this, in order to keep the distinctions between the experimental treatments as sharp as possible.

Three reasons can be suggested for the results. Cazden originally proposed that richness of verbal stimulation might be more important than the grammatical contingency of the adult response. If we consider the learning of syntactic rules to be akin to concept formation, then learning may be aided by variation in non-criterial attributes — for instance, the particular noun stem in the case of inflection for plurality. If the process of first language learning is akin to construction of scientific theory, in which hypotheses are tested against available data, then a meager set of data may be disadvantageous. We have seen that bias in the mother-to-child sampling of the possibilities of English grammar caused Adam to make the segmentation error revealed in such a sentence as *It's fell.*

Miller and McNeill (in press) suggest an alternative explanation. When an adult attempts to expand a child's telegraphic utterances far more often than parents spontaneously do, some of the expansions probably misinterpret the child's intended meaning. Instead of facilitating the acquisition of grammar, such erroneous expansions may mislead the child and interfere with his learning.

Still a third explanation is possible, separately or in conjunction with either of the previous two. Artificial elevation of the expansion rate may depress attentional processes in the child. We know from many current studies of child development that stimuli of a certain degree of novelty — not too familar and not too strange — command the greatest attention. The acquisition of language should be facilitated by those environmental events that enhance the child's attention to the adult's utterance and to relevant features of the verbal and nonverbal context in which it is spoken. In these particular experimental treatments, a greater degree of novelty may have been attained in the modeling treatment. We do not consider this experiment conclusive; all we can say is that the benefits of expansions remain unproved.

TRAINING VARIABLES IN THE LONGITUDINAL DATA

In the last two years we have gone back to the longitudinal data on Adam, Eve, and Sarah to look more carefully for evidence of the effects of parental speech. In selecting dependent variables, we have learned to reject measures of the child's performance in favor of better indicators of the child's grammatical knowledge. We have substantive findings on the independent variables of expansions and modeling, occasional questions, and expressions of approval and disapproval.

Grammatical Knowledge versus Performance. In certain facts about construction frequency there lies a major trap for the student of child speech who is interested in the development of knowledge of grammar: the first fact is that in mother-to-child speech the various constructions that English grammar permits are of grossly unequal frequency; the second is that the frequencies are astonishingly stable across the three mothers in our study; and the third is that frequencies in child speech, within the limits of the child's competence, tend to match adult frequencies. We have examined frequencies on many levels, from major types of sentence all the way down to the several allomorphs of *be*, and the story is always the same: rank order correlations among the mothers and between each mother and her child ranging from .65 to .90.

Some of the stable inequalities one might have guessed: active affirmative, declarative sentences are much more common than negatives, yes-no interrogatives, or wh interrogatives, and well-formed passives are almost nonexistent. Others are easy to understand but are not likely to have occurred to anyone who has not counted: the impersonal pronouns *it, this,* and *that* as sentence subjects almost always have their allomorph of *be* (*is*) as verb, whereas the personal pronouns *I, you, he,* and so forth as subjects have a main verb much more often than an allomorph of *be; where* questions are very much more frequent than *when* or *how* or *why* questions; catenative semi-auxiliaries like *wanna* and *gonna* are much more frequent than the modal auxiliaries *will* or *can,* and *may* and *must* are seldom heard; the progressive inflection *-ing* is much more frequent than the regular past *-ed,* and irregular pasts (e.g., *ran, saw, did*) are more frequent than regular pasts; and so on. The important general fact is that there seems to be something like a standard frequency profile for mother-to-child English, a profile that children match within their competence at any given time, and in this profile great inequalities exist even among very simple and familiar constructions.

Consider two examples in detail: major sentence types and expressions of possession. If we set an arbitrary frequency in child speech as a criterion of emergence — for example, the occurrence of three instances of a given type of sentence in each of three consecutive samples of seven hundred utterances — we find a high rank order correlation between parental frequencies and order of emergence in the child for twenty-four types of sentence — affirmative, declaratives, negatives, yes-no interrogatives, and wh interrogatives using, respectively, lexical verbs or *have* or *be* or *will* or *can* or *may*. Lexical and *be*-verbs in declarative sentences are the most common in all three mothers and appear first in the speech of all three children. But suppose we entertain the extreme hypothesis that all twenty-four verbs enter the child's competence simultaneously. Because the probability that a given construction will attain an arbitrary criterion varies with its standard frequency in mother-to-child English, and because these frequencies are grossly unequal, lexical and *be*-verbs would appear first on a strict probability basis. The student of child speech might then conclude that the hypothesis of simultaneous development was false when it could indeed still be true. Highly stable orders of construction emergence, in terms of an arbitrary frequency criterion, are not inconsistent with the possibility that the children in question know how to form all the constructions from the start but produce them with unequal frequency.

The same misleading performance match appears when we relate individual differences in construction frequencies among the children to differences in their mothers' speech. For instance, one of the first individual differences we noted was Eve's tendency to use N + N constructions far more often than Adam or Sarah did. At I, the frequencies of N + N in 700 utterances were: Eve, 66; Adam, 40; Sarah, 10, of which 8 were imitations. In looking for an explanation, we thought it possible that the speech of the three mothers might differ in the frequency with which sentences were spoken from which N + N constructions might be telegraphically derived. The best match to the rank order of the children was the particular subset of parental N + N constructions that express possession, such as *Daddy's chair*. In the first 1,253 utterances of each mother, these frequencies were: Eve's mother, 31; Adam's mother, 24; Sarah's mother, only 6. This is an extremely interesting relation. One can hypothesize that territoriality and property rights are more important in homes where father is a graduate student, and that this is related to the child's tendency to use the N + N construction. But it is not sufficient evidence that greater frequency in parent speech produces earlier learning in the child. It is the antecedents of grammatical *knowledge* we are seeking, not influences on performance.

There are various ways out of the trap, all involving data that are better indexes of knowledge or competence than is an arbitrary frequency of production. One can consider child frequencies against a background of known stable adult frequencies and so set frequency criteria that are not entirely arbitrary; one can consider frequencies of forms in contexts that make them obligatory; one can consider the pattern of omissions in the total distributional range of a form; one can consider the adequacy of the child's responses to adult questions and assertions; and above all, one can use the child's analogical errors of commission. In analyses of the relation of child speech to parental speech, the frequency of forms in contexts that make them obligatory has proved an especially useful measure. Each of these contexts in the child's speech can be considered a learning trial, and we can compute the proportion of times in which the child performs appropriately as that proportion changes over time.

Further Evidence on Expansions and Modeling. Because we considered the manipulative experiment inconclusive, we have probed further into the effect of expansions and modeling on the growth of specific aspects of grammatical knowledge in our three subjects. We have charted the emergence of prepositions in Eve's speech and of appropriate answers to four kinds of wh questions and five noun and verb inflections in all three children.

Table 5 presents the data for the emergence of Eve's prepositions. Two findings are of interest: First, for any given preposition, both the frequency with which it is modeled and the frequency (but not proportion) of expansions are strongly related to the point at which that preposition is regularly supplied by the child in all the phrases requiring it. In Samples 1–6,

Table 5. Eve's Performance in Supplying Various Prepositions in
Samples 7–12 Compared with Eve's Mother's Modeling
Frequencies and Expansions in Samples 1–6

Preposition	Mother's Modeling Frequencies 1–6	Mother's Proportion of Expansions 1–6	Proportion Correct in Eve 7–12
On	157	.57 (25/44)	.90 (82/92)
In	142	.61 (20/33)	.92 (147/159)
With	54	.64 (7/11)	.67 (29/43)
Of	33	.50 (1/2)	.70 (14/20)
For	32	.40 (2/5)	.69 (11/16)
To	31	.00 (0/3)	.78 (7/9)

Eve's mother uses *in* and *on* approximately three times as often as she uses *with, of, for,* or *to.* In Samples 7–12, Eve supplies *in* and *on* correctly at least 90 per cent of the time, and the proportion correct for each of the other four prepositions is between .67 and .77.

Second, there is no relation at all between modeling frequency of particular phrases — *in there* versus *in the wastebasket* — and the point at which the child produces that phrase with the preposition in place. A given preposition appears in all the phrases requiring it at about the same time, and it does not matter whether the particular phrase has been often modeled by the mother or not. This is a good example of how parental speech aids the induction of general rules but does not provide models for imitation as such.

With wh questions, we can determine what proportion of a given type elicits semantically and grammatically appropriate answers from the child. Four wh-adverbial questions are rather well matched in grammatical (though probably not in semantic) complexity, but they differ greatly in parental frequency. For all three mothers at II, the order of frequency is locatives first (about three fourths of the total), then causal, manner, and time — in other words, *where, why, how,* and *when.* This rank order matches the rank order of proportion of appropriate responses from the children at V except for questions about time, for which the data are too few to be reliable. Pooled data for the three mothers and children are presented in the accompanying tabulation.

	Frequency of Mothers' Questions	*Proportion of Children's Appropriate Responses*
Locative	228	.64 (29/45)
Causal	29	.40 (14/35)
Manner	18	.11 (1/9)
Time	7	.50 (1/2)

Before turning to the emergence of inflections, another comment on method is in order. For relating child behavior to parental behavior in a sample of more than one child, two approaches are possible. The child's language can be related to antecedents in his parent's speech, and this relation then compared across the dyads; no direct comparison of the children is made. The preceding analyses of twenty-four verb forms, prepositions, and answers to wh questions were of this type. Alternatively, differences in the language of the children can be related to differences in the language of their parents. The preceding analysis of N + N constructions was of this type. Here, direct comparison of the children is required, and the experimenter faces the question of a metric for that comparison. We have analyzed the emergence of inflections in both ways.

The five regular inflections which emerge between I and V are the plural and possessive inflections on the noun and the present progressive, regular past, and present indicative inflections on the verb. For this analysis we used as a criterion of emergence the first sample of three, such that, in all three, the child supplies the inflection in at least 90 per cent of the contexts in which they are clearly required. The charting of this aspect of development is a long story in itself and will be reported in detail elsewhere. We shall describe here only the data for the correlations between the sequence of emergence and three features of the child's linguistic environment: the proportion of times in which his omitted inflections are expanded by the parent during the entire period I–V, the absolute frequency of those expansions, and the frequency with which the inflections are modeled in four samples of seven hundred parental utterances which immediately precede Levels II, III, IV, and V of the children's speech.

First, we computed rank-order correlations for each child separately. For all three children, order of emergence within the child's language system is more strongly related to the frequency with which the inflection is modeled by the parent than it is to the proportion or frequency of expansions. The only statistically significant positive correlation is with frequency of modeling for Sarah, $\rho = .90$ ($p < .05$).

We have also looked for relations between differences among the children and differences among their parents. It is here that a metric for comparing the children is required. In the above analysis of N + N constructions, the three children were compared at II; the metric, therefore, was mean length of utterance. A more conventional metric is age. We have analyzed individual differences in the order of emergence of inflections on both bases of comparison — the contrast in outcomes is itself informative.

When we compare the children on the basis of age, the order of development is what one would expect from the figure on page 29: Eve way out in front, Adam second, and Sarah third. But when we ignore age and compare the children on the basis of mean length, the rank order of the children changes sharply. At II, when all three children have a mean length of 2.25 morphemes, only Sarah has reached the 90 per cent criterion on any inflection (plurality). By IV, when mean length has increased to 3.50 morphemes, she has reached criterion on five inflections, Eve has on four, and Adam on two. Data tabulated independently for the percentage of missing functors (everything except nouns, verbs, adjectives, and adverbs) at II and V yield the same relation: for Eve, 81 per cent of the functors were missing at II and 43 per cent at V; for Adam, 83 per cent at II, 20 per cent at V; and for Sarah, 74 per cent at II, 15 per cent at V.

Looked at in this way, the relative position of Eve and Sarah is reversed. At any given mean length value for utterances, Sarah is handling inflections and functors in general more successfully than Eve. Conversely, since Eve's speech contains proportionately more content words than Sarah's, her utterances are more informative. Eve had undoubtedly caught up in the provision of functors by the time she reached Sarah's age, probably well before. The point is that Sarah is less behind in the provision of obligatory functors than in what she is trying to say.

Table 6 shows the relation between order of emergence of the five inflections on these two bases of comparison (age and mean length) and proportion and frequency of expansions and frequency of modeling in parent speech.

Table 6. Emergence of Inflections and Two Features of Parental Speech

Child's Speech	Eve	Adam	Sarah
Inflections			
Order of emergence,[a] by age	5	12.5	12.5
Order of emergence,[a] by mean length.	11	12	7
Proportion of parental expansions	.45	.51	.29
	(191/427)	(348/679)	86/294)
Frequency of parental models	499	576	471

[a] Order of emergence is given in summed ranks which range from 5 to 15 — first to last of the three children on the five inflections combined.

As one would expect from the previous discussion of mother-child communication patterns, the difference in modeling frequency among the parents is small. But the difference in proportion and frequency of expansions is considerable: Sarah's telegraphic utterances omitting inflections are followed much less frequently by a parent utterance including the appropriate inflection than are Adam's and Eve's. This we expected from our observation of differential expansion rates at the beginning of our work. What is surprising is the negative relation between expansion rate and order of emergence in terms of mean length of utterance. Sarah receives the lowest density of expansions, yet her language system is relatively the most advanced in the provision of inflections. It is hard to reconcile this finding with our original hypothesis that expansions should provide the most usable information for the acquisition of all types of functors.

Expressions of Approval and Disapproval. It might be supposed that syntactically correct utterances come to prevail over those that are incorrect through the operation of positive reinforcement and punishment on the part of adults. Because events subsequent to a child's speech are infinitely various, one can never be sure that there is no event which functions as a reinforcer or punishment. In practice, however, we know that certain events such as signs of approval or disapproval are likely to function in this way. The proposition "Syntactically correct utterances come to prevail over syntactically incorrect utterances through the selective administration of signs of approval and disapproval" is a testable one.

The proposition cannot be true for the natural case of parents and children at home unless parental approval and disapproval are in fact appropriately contingent on syntactical correctness. If the reactions *are* appropriately contingent, then they may or may not have the effects proposed. For this analysis, we worked with samples II and V. The general plan was to contrast the syntactic correctness of the population of utterances followed by a sign of approval — *that's right, very good*, or just *yes* — with the population of utterances followed by a sign of disapproval — *that's wrong* or *no*. The results are simply stated: there is not a shred of evidence that approval and disapproval are contingent on syntactic correctness.

What circumstances did govern approval and disapproval directed at child utterances by parents? Gross errors of word choice were sometimes corrected, as when Eve said *What the guy idea.* Once in a while an error of pronunciation was noticed and corrected. Most commonly, however, the grounds on which an utterance was approved or disapproved in Levels I — V were not strictly linguistic at all. When Eve expressed the opinion that her mother was a girl by saying *He a girl*, her mother answered *That's right.* The child's utterance was ungrammatical, but her mother did not respond to that fact; instead, she responded to the truth of the proposition the child intended to express. In general, the parents fitted propositions to the child's utterances, however incomplete or distorted the utterances, and then approved or not according to the correspondence between proposition and reality. Thus, *Her curl my hair* was approved because the mother was, in fact, curling Eve's hair. However, Sarah's grammatically impeccable *There's the animal farmhouse* was disapproved because the building was a lighthouse, and Adam's *Walt Disney comes on on Tuesday* was disapproved because Walt Disney came on on some other day. It seems, then, to be truth value rather than syntactic well-formedness that chiefly governs explicit verbal reinforcement by parents — which renders mildly paradoxical the fact that the usual product of such a training schedule is an adult whose speech is highly grammatical but not notably truthful.

Interaction Routines with Occasional Questions. In describing the systematic relations that underlie the grammar of wh questions, we introduced in Table 2 the forms called occasional questions because we believe they are a great help in making those relations clear in explicit form to adults. We naturally wonder, therefore, whether the occasional questions also help make the relations clear in implicit form to children. The mothers of Adam, Eve, and Sarah produced such questions in two circumstances, which may be represented as follows: First, *say constituent again* — (a) Child, "I want milk," Mother, "You want what?" Child, "Milk." or (b) Child, "Put milk in glass." Mother, "Put milk where?" Child, "In glass." Second, *constituent prompt* — (a) Mother, "What do you want?" Child, no answer. Mother, "You want what?" or (b) Mother, "Where will I put it?" Child, no answer. Mother, "I will put it where?"

The say-constituent-again interaction occurred when mother found a part of a child's utterance unintelligible. She then repeated what she had understood and replaced the constituent which was the locus of unintelligibility with the right kind of wh word. Since the wh word appeared in the sentence position of a constituent, the result was an occasional question. The occasion was unintelligibility in a constituent, and the child's response was repetition of the constituent displaced. The mother's question is essentially a request to say the constituent again and that is the name we have given to this kind of interaction. What should such exchanges be able to teach the child? Perhaps, the membership of each type of sentence constituent — members of NP, for example, are just those terms, of whatever complexity, that can be replaced by *what*.

The constituent-prompt interaction was initiated by the mother. She asked a question in the normal form — "What do you want?" — and received no answer. She then reformulated the question as "You want what?" which is, incidentally, an occasional question. She was, in effect, turning the question into a sentence completion item, and since the mothers usually resorted to this prompting form when the normal form had failed,

71

they must have felt that it was easier to process. In our materials, the occasional form was, in fact, more likely to elicit an appropriate answer than was the normal form. What should exchanges of this type be able to teach the child? Fundamentally, the equivalence of particular normal and occasional questions — equivalents are questions that replace one another when no answer is forthcoming.

A large amount of structural information is revealed in these two interactions with unusual clarity because of the use of the occasional question. It must be possible to discover the systematic relations that underlie the grammar of wh questions without the benefit of the occasional question, since many children who learn English do not have attentive mothers around to echo and prompt them. However, it may be easier to discover the relations if the middle term is often heard. It may be accidental, but in our records, the occasional form was used much more frequently by the mothers of the two children whose grammatical understanding developed more rapidly, Adam and Eve: in samples of seven thousand parental utterances, Adam's mother produced occasional questions at the rate of 1 in 57 utterances; Eve's mother at the rate of 1 in 80; Sarah's mother at the rate of only 1 in 146.

Whether or not the occasional questions prove to be helpful for the discovery of wh grammar, it seems likely that the many kinds of grammatical exchange in discourse will prove to be the richest data available to the child in his search for a grammar. It may be as difficult to derive a grammar from hearing unconnected static sentences as it would be to derive the invariance of quantity and number from simply looking at liquids in containers and objects in space. The changes produced by pouring back and forth and by gathering together and spreading apart are the data that most strongly suggest the conservation of quantity and number. We suspect that the changes sentences undergo as they shuttle between persons in conversation are, similarly, the data that most clearly expose the underlying structure of language.

We have examined the effect on the child's development of grammatical knowledge of two aspects of the speech he hears: variation in the frequency with which particular constructions are modeled and variation in the frequency of particular parental responses — expansions, expressions of approval and disapproval, and occasional questions. There is a small amount of evidence that modeling frequency does affect the acquisition of knowledge. With regard to the parental responses of expansion and approval-disapproval, the present evidence is that neither has any effect on the development of grammatical knowledge. The role of occasional questions is still unknown. Our own interest in isolated training variables is giving way to an interest in the structural information latent in various forms of linguistic interaction. Perhaps we shall someday find that linguistic environments at home do vary significantly in structural richness but that any single form of response is an unreliable index of this variation, even as age of weaning has proved an unreliable index of something more important — general child-rearing attitudes.

References

Brown, R. The development of wh questions in child speech. *Journal of Verbal Learning and Verbal Behavior.* In press, 1968.

———, & Ursula Bellugi. Three processes in the child's acquisition of syntax. *Harvard Educational Review*, 1964, 34, 133–151.

Brown, R., & C. Fraser. The acquisition of syntax, in C. N. Cofer & Barbara S. Musgrave, eds. *Verbal behavior and learning*, pp. 158–197. New York: McGraw-Hill, 1963.

Cazden, Courtney B. Environmental assistance to the child's acquisition of grammar. Ph.D. thesis, Harvard Univer., 1965.

Chomsky, N. *Syntactic structures.* The Hague: Mouton, 1957.

———. *Aspects of the theory of syntax.* Cambridge, Mass.: M.I.T. Press, 1965.

Fodor, J. A. How to learn to talk: Some simple ways, in F. Smith & G. A. Miller, eds. *The genesis of language*, pp. 105–122. Cambridge, Mass.: M.I.T. Press, 1966.

Gleason, H. A. *An introduction to descriptive linguistics*, rev. ed. New York: Holt, 1961.

Harris, Z. S. Morpheme alternates in linguistic analysis. *Language*, 1942, 18, 169–180.

———. *Methods in structural linguistics.* Chicago: University of Chicago Press, 1951.

Heffner, R. M. S. *General phonetics.* Madison: University of Wisconsin Press, 1949.

Hockett, C. F. Problems of morphemic analysis. *Language*, 1947, 23, 321–43.

Katz, J. J., & P. M. Postal. *An integrated theory of linguistic descriptions.* Cambridge, Mass.: M.I.T. Press, 1964.

Klima, E. S. Negation in English, in J. A. Fodor & J. J. Katz, eds. *The structure of language: Readings in the philosophy of language*, pp. 246–323. Englewood Cliffs, N.J.: Prentice-Hall, 1964.

McNeill, D. Developmental psycholinguistics, in F. Smith & G. A. Miller, eds. *The genesis of language*, pp. 15–84. Cambridge, Mass.: M.I.T. Press, 1966.

Miller, G. A., & D. McNeill. Psycholinguistics, in G. Lindzey & E. Arsonson, eds. *Handbook of social psychology.* Reading, Mass.: Addison-Wesley, 1968.

Nida, E. S. The identification of morphemes. *Language*, 1948, 24, 414–441.

Slobin, D. I. The acquisition of Russian as a native language, in F. Smith & G. A. Miller, eds. *The genesis of language*, pp. 129–148. Cambridge, Mass.: M.I.T. Press, 1966.

Spitz, R. A. *No and yes: On the genesis of human communication.* New York: International Universities Press, 1957.

◈ BETTYE M. CALDWELL ◈

A New "Approach" to Behavioral Ecology

CHILD psychology generally is designated as having had an official existence from the time of the publication of a few diaries or baby biographies. These diaries represented early attempts at the compilation of human ecological data. That is, the authors relied upon their own powers of observation to assimilate naturally occurring behavioral events, and they made an attempt to relate behavior to the existing environmental conditions. It was the custom for many years to condemn such biographies as biased and unscientific; yet anyone who has read even excerpts from the reports of Darwin (1877) or Preyer (1888) might question that generalization. In retrospect, they appear to represent careful exercise of scientific caution and restraint and the utmost respect for accuracy and detail. Such biographies are analogous to the careful descriptions of clinical material which have played a major role in the advancement of medical science and to the description of naturally occurring phenomena in botany and astronomy.

Wright (1960) has commented that psychology moved quickly from the armchair to the laboratory, preferring "to do things with its subjects, to give them tasks or problems, to interrogate them, to test them, or at least to draw them into prearranged situations" (1960, pp. 71–72). This leap into the laboratory may have resulted in part from a legitimate attempt to help psychology "catch up" with the physical sciences, rather than with any aversion to the fairly long observe-and-record stage through

NOTE: The author wishes to acknowledge the contributions of her colleagues Alice S. Honig, Jordan Tannenbaum, and Ruth L. Wynn to the work reported in this paper. The work reported has been supported by Grant No. D-156(R), Children's Bureau Social and Rehabilitation Services, and Grant No. MH-07649, National Institutes of Health, Department of Health, Education, and Welfare.

which most other areas of science have progressed and from which some have little hope of emerging.

Before a comprehensive theory of human behavior can be formulated, the annals of behavioral science will need to contain large numbers of descriptions of freely varying behavior occurring within freely constituted environments. For certain types of problems with which the field of child development is currently concerned, there is simply no substitute for meticulous naturalistic studies of children functioning in different environmental settings. My own interest in this task stemmed from research in the area of early childhood learning and patterns of environmental care. Such an assignment calls for simultaneous assessment of various parameters of individual development and of the environment in which the learning will occur. Although a great deal of attention has been paid to the development of newer and better techniques for assessing one or another aspect of the learning process, relatively little has been devoted to the task of measuring the environments in which learning occurs.

There are several deterrents to ecological research in human behavior. One is simply that most scientists are committed to the superiority of the laboratory method for answering most of the major questions of concern to the field. Such a conviction carries the inference that the influence of environmental variables can be best understood by selective control of these variables — that is, by contriving to produce certain magnitudes of the variables under study and then observing their effects on the dependent variables. Implicit in this approach is the idea that field tests under naturally occurring levels of the environmental variables can be more profitable after more rigorous laboratory studies have provided evidence on which variables are important.

A second deterrent to the conduct of such studies is the cost in both time and money. Naturalistic observation of events in situ generally will produce a great deal of surplus information that does not necessarily relate to topics of major interest for the investigator. And yet these must also consume their share of attention and effort. Thus, the extravagance of this approach to behavior study easily can make an investigator nostalgic for methods in which a little careful staging of events and internal conditions will increase the probability that high interest behaviors will predominate in the record.

But undoubtedly, the major deterrent to the compilation of large numbers of samples of behavior in situ has been the dilemma of what to do

75

with such records after they have been obtained. Do they get typed up and filed away "for future reference"? Do they get rated on selected variables? And, if so, why not simply rate the behavior while it is being observed and skip the laborious step of recording and transcribing it first? Does one select only certain portions of the record for analysis? But, most naggingly, how does one go about the overwhelming task of reducing the data to manageable proportions and of converting it into either enumerative or numerical form for analysis and synthesis? Generally, this task has required the development of some sort of coding system for the conversion process, and the development of a coding system sensitive enough and elaborate enough to relay the complexities of human behavior is in itself a formidable task. Many such coding systems have appeared, have attracted a few students and disciples, and perhaps have serviced the research conducted within one or two laboratories. But none has had the versatility or appeal to attract workers in different settings to use the same coding system and thus facilitate comparison of obtained results.

In the present paper I wish to introduce a new method for translating data from records of behavior in situ into a numerical code which is eminently suitable for computer summarization and analysis. Developed by Caldwell, Honig, and Wynn (1967), the method has been called AP-PROACH — A Procedure for Patterning Responses of Adults and Children. No claim is made that it will possess the necessary qualifications for a universal coding system or even that the format developed will appeal to other workers. Nor has it been tried and tested sufficiently within our own laboratory to convince us that its format will survive intact as it is applied in more and different settings. However, it is a workable system, fairly easily learned, and capable of being adapted to almost any kind of behavioral record that one might wish to prepare for data analysis. Development of such a scheme is enormously time-consuming; the present one consumed significant portions of think-time for three people for almost two years, with a germination period for me of some seven years before the active work period. It is my conviction that anyone wishing to develop a similar schema would have to commit similarly large blocks of time to its formulation and refinement. As such massive efforts significantly reduce the amount of time which can then be devoted to applications of the method, it appeared reasonable to introduce the present formulation to the scientific community in the hope that others with ecological interests might find it potentially useful.

BETTYE M. CALDWELL

Development of the APPROACH Method

The most persuasive case for the need for more ecological studies of human behavior has been made by Barker and Wright (1949; 1954) and their associates over the years, and I am indebted to this group for infecting me with enthusiasm for the task. My own theoretical orientation, however, stems more from the tradition exemplified in an early paper by Sears (1951), concerned with the development of a diadic behavior model. In this, the behavior of one member of the diad was conceptualized as comprising the environmental events to which the other member of the diad must react. There is no conflict between this model and ecological goals, of course, since other people generally represent the most significant components of the environment likely to be studied in any ecological analysis.

But ecological studies cannot stop with social diads, for individual-environment interaction is often polyadic rather than simply diadic — this is always the case whenever behavior occurs in any group of more than two. Therefore, a method, in order to be useful for ecological analysis, should permit information to be organized around some one individual but take in significant details about all the other people and objects with whom and which he interacts. This, in a capsule, expresses the general objective of the task of devising a behavioral coding system.

SPECIFIC REQUIREMENTS OF THE CODING PROCEDURE

In addition to the general objective of the planned coding procedure, my colleagues and I also formulated several more specific requirements of the planned system, some of which follow:

a. The system should not only describe the behavior of the central figure of the observation but also report all the significant behaviors directed to the central figure, or even salient behaviors that occur in his vicinity and to which he could be expected to react. Thus, for true ecological analysis, a coding system needs to describe behavior within settings, with the settings themselves defined to cover behavioral events and significant features of the physical environment.

b. The system should adequately handle the behavior of a person in any type of social grouping (monads, diads, polyads) and any type of social setting (informal play, formal learning situations, mealtimes, etc.). This is essential if the method is to be applied to such ecological problems as differences in behavior as a function of social setting (e.g., play behavior as a function of size of play group) or locale (behavior in nursery school compared with behavior at home).

c. The same behavior categories should apply to all members of the social grouping, thus avoiding the clumsiness and redundancy involved in such compromises as separate sets of categories for children and for adults. If the system could achieve this objective, there would also be no problem about applicability across all ages of childhood, a chronic problem for persons interested in child development. That is, all too many measuring instruments available for child study stop at some arbitrary age boundary (e.g., one must use one developmental test with infants up to age two and a different one with children two or older) and create serious problems of measurement continuity at the interfaces.

d. The system should permit detailed analyses of sequences of behavior, both between and within individuals. For example, what kinds of child behaviors follow a series of adult commands or requests? What kinds of adult behaviors follow noncompliance and what kinds follow compliance? What kinds of adult behaviors follow adult commands delivered in a preemptory fashion as opposed to a more permissive style? What kinds of child behaviors follow a series of child assaults on another person? How does a change of setting influence such sequences? These represent only the smallest fraction of questions about the intra- and inter-individual sequencing of behavior that need to be studied and understood. It is my conviction that only a method which permits detailed and meticulous delineation of behavioral events will permit a meaningful investigation of such questions.

e. The system should be able to describe the contributions to the stimulus field made by nonhuman objects as well as by people. A great deal of the interaction between persons and environment is with objects; this is as true of the young child as it is of adults. Likewise, many of the stimuli that elicit a reaction from a person are emitted by objects within the environment. Thus it is as meaningful to know that a child ran to look out a window upon hearing a fire siren as it is to know that he looked toward a door upon hearing a particular voice from the doorway.

f. The system should be convertible to a simple numerical code for rapid reading, summarization, and data analysis by computers. Unless the system required memorization of only a small number of categories (as in Flanders' ten-category system, 1965), most previous techniques with which I am acquainted have used some sort of alphabetic abbreviation for the shorthand coding symbols. Good examples of this may be found in Bishop (1951) and Gewirtz (1962). This type of symbolization appeared to be an unnecessary step in the translation process, and a decision was made to go directly from behavior record to numbers. In the light of the eventual scheme of using columnar placement of numbers and the separation of similar behavior into deciles, the direct number designation has proven no more difficult to memorize than an alphabetic code and has saved one step in the transmission of information to the computer.

g. The system should not be too complicated to be learned fairly quickly and to be used and coded reliably. If one is fairly lenient on one's definition of the words "complicated" and "quickly" in the above statement, then perhaps the APPROACH system fulfils this requirement — but only marginally. There was originally a second component to this aim, namely, that the coding system would permit "live" translation from ongoing behavior to coded record without the intervening step of any sort of verbal or written record. At this stage, this has never been achieved, and it is unlikely that it ever will be without some loss of the information that is now carefully put into the analytic record. However, we are learning to code quite satisfactorily from tapes, thus bypassing the expensive and time-consuming step of transcribing the protocols.

THE BEHAVIOR SAMPLE

For any type of observational study, some decision must be made about the type of behavior sample to be obtained and about the units which will be used for analysis. In what is undoubtedly the best summary of available methods, Wright (1960) lists six techniques from which an investigator may choose: diary description, specimen description, time sampling, event sampling, field unit analysis, and trait rating. From this possible array, we opted for specimen description as most closely fitting our research aims. Wright (1960, pp. 83–84) defines this method as follows:

This method begins with the scheduled and continuous observing and narrative recording of a behavior sequence under chosen conditions of time and life setting. A child to observe and a time and particular place in which to observe are selected to suit special interests. But the observer in the field is in no way deliberately selective. He is instead deliberately unselective in the sense that he aims to make a faithful record of "everything" as it comes in the behavior and situation of the child . . . The recorded material is usually subjected to study that varies among different applications from ever so free interpretation to somewhat strict and thorough-going quantitative analysis.

Almost any other type of record could have satisfied all our research requirements except the utility of the method for sequential analysis of behavior. If behavior sequences are to be analyzed, then continuous recording for some specified period of time is essential. To date, all our records have been either 30-minute or 20-minute samples chosen from times of day most likely to contain certain activities which we wished to observe. However, plans are currently being made for full-day records, for on-off 10-minute records throughout an available day, and for simultaneous records made on several children within the same setting. The model is versatile enough to be applicable to any and all such specimen records.

OBTAINING THE BEHAVIOR RECORD

The behavior record is obtained by having an observer station himself near the person being observed and whisper into a small portable tape recorder all the significant behaviors emitted by the central figure and all the behaviors directed toward the central figure. In the ordinarily noisy classroom or home, the minimal voice volume picked up by a sensitive microphone will not be audible even a foot away from the observer. This high-visibility method has been chosen in preference to such techniques as having a child wear a microphone which transmits to an FM receiver and to having the observer stationed in a one-way observation room. For our purposes, the implanted microphone proved to be totally unacceptable, since it preserved indiscriminately every dropped toy and every verbalization of the subject, with the latter usually coming through with less fidelity and comprehensibility. In addition, such a technique required the dictation of a simultaneous record which described both the child's behavior and the setting in which it was occurring. Similarly, stationing observers behind a one-way mirror would have required, in our setting, restriction of the mobility of the children to certain areas of the school. Also, it would have meant that samples obtained in homes, where one-way mirrors are seldom standard pieces of equipment, would not have been methodologically comparable.

The procedure of stationing the observer right in the geographic area where the behavior is occurring has worked quite successfully. It permits records to be made in hallways, on the playground, on the school bus, and in any other area in which the child or adult might circulate. Our policy is to make a few minutes of a dummy recording at the beginning of an observation period. Even this soon becomes unnecessary, however, as the children in the program quickly learn to tune out an unresponsive adult. Unless an observer sees a child in imminent danger and knows that no other teacher or caretaker is looking, he or she does not intervene in the ongoing behavior in any way. Our observers are, quite literally, pieces of movable equipment. The descriptive record so obtained is transcribed, and, currently, all coding is done from the typescripts.

The APPROACH Model

There are two major divisions of the APPROACH system, one devoted to a delineation of a meaningful array of *behaviors* likely to be emitted by young children and the adults who interact with them and the other to some of the most characteristic *settings* in which these behaviors might occur. Each of these divisions is coded in a similar way — that is, the information is converted to a five-digit numerical statement. However, because the type of information conveyed in these two major divisions of the code is quite different, the behavior codes and the setting codes are discussed separately.

EMITTED BEHAVIORS

Any transformation from narrative description to a code involves some sort of unitizing of the obtained record. The resulting units of behavior may be classified along a dimension from microscopic to macroscopic. The present system handles the unitizing problem, usually one which causes much distress and unreliability in the coding process, quite effortlessly and, in the process, automates decisions about how microscopic the behavioral units should be. The coding model involves breaking up the described emitted behaviors into behavioral clauses, with each unit being basically designated by the appearance in the record of a verb. Every time a verb is used by the observer, someone has done something; and that action, small or large, is coded. Each behavioral clause (Johnny looks at his teacher) is thus described in terms of four basic components — the *subject* of the clause (who or what does something), the *predicate* or action of the clause (what is done), the *object* of the clause (toward whom or what the action is directed), and a few selected *qualifiers* (adverbs) which provide supplementary information. Each of these four components of the behavioral clause is then translated into a numerical code and grouped into a five-digit statement (two digits are required for the complete array of predicates) which summarizes the subject-predicate-object-adverb involved in a single behavior unit. The complete chain of numerical statements is then keypunched for computer analysis.

Each of the behavioral "parts of speech" has been carefully defined and delimited. Space does not permit presentation of the complete definition of each component. However, any use of the system would require careful study of the definitions. For this the reader is referred to the APPROACH coding manual (Caldwell et al., 1967). In this paper each of the components of the behavioral language will be introduced with sufficient detail to permit the presentation of data exemplifying the application of the method to ecological analysis.

Subject of the Behavioral Clause. For most purposes, the number of different subjects needed will be fewer than ten, thus making it necessary to assign only one column to the subject. In the present format, information about the subject is conveyed in the first digit of the numerical statement.

0   Central Figure (CF) of the observation. It may be either a child or an adult; in all our studies to date it has been a child.
1   Environment. Stationary items in the physical-spatial environment.
2   Female Adult. Any female assuming adult responsibility in the situation.
3   Female Child. Any female child other than the CF (assuming the CF is female).
4   Item. Any portable or manipulable item or article of household or play equipment.
5   Male Child. Any male child other than the CF (assuming CF is male).
6   Group, including the CF. Two or more people, either adults, children, or a combination, which includes the CF of the observation.
7   Group, excluding the CF. Two or more people, not including the CF.
8   Male Adult. Any male assuming adult responsibility in the situation.
9   Setting Alert. This is the only initial digit which does not identify the subject of an emitted behavior clause. It announces that all codes between this and the next statement beginning with 9 refer to behavior occurring within a specific type of setting (to be defined later). The first statement in all coded records should thus begin with a 9.

If a greater variety of subjects should be desired — for example, if all the children and adults in a particular nursery school setting need to be identified by name rather than merely as male or female child or adult – then one must establish code numbers for all individuals and change the model from a five- to a seven-digit statement. This can be accomplished with no distress to computer programs set up for analyzing the data translated into the APPROACH code.

Behavioral Predicates. There are more verbs than any other parts of behavioral speech in the APPROACH code; therefore, two columns of digits (the second and third) are regularly used to report the action. In order for reliable coding to be done, it is imperative that full definitions of all predicates, as given in the APPROACH manual, be carefully studied. To facilitate learning, the numerals assigned to represent different predicates have been grouped into numerical regions. They will be introduced below in this numerical order. The predicates necessary to describe child and adult behavior in the settings we have studied to date cover some nine areas: environmental contact, information processing, food behavior, manual activities, negative reinforcement, positive reinforcement, body activities, miscellaneous verbs and control techniques.

Environmental contact (00–04). This area covers behaviors involving the attentiveness of observed subjects and the degree of visual and auditory contact maintained with people, items, or events in the environment.

00 Ignores. The person described is unresponsive to some person, object, or event.
01 Attends. The actor attends to a stimulus.
02 Establishes or maintains contact. One person moves or acts in such a way as to perpetuate contact with another person.
03 Terminates contact. One person turns or walks away from another person or activity.
04 Scans. The subject looks about the environment for some particular person or object.

Information Processing (10–19). This category covers all informational interchanges between persons.

10 Confirms. Information that a person's behavior is appropriate or correct is given.
11 Shows. Transmission of skills or information via gesture or demonstration.
12 Converses. Brief or casual statements relating to routine situations.
13 Writes or draws. Subject writes or prints words or uses crayon or pencil for representational drawing.
14 Reads to. Subject reads from a book to one or more persons.

15   Corrects or disconfirms. Subject corrects false information.
16   Inquires. Subject asks a question, the answer to which involves substantive information.
17   Informs or teaches. Subject gives, in somewhat formal manner, information to another person.
18   Informs about culture. Subject relates information about rules of behavior.
19   Role plays. Subject transcends factual informational exchange in creative way.

Food Behavior (20–24). Various actions having to do with feeding, ingestion, manipulation, or disorganization with food.

20   Gives food (to). Activity relating to serving or ingesting of food.
21   Takes or handles food. Subject takes food with his hands from some spot in the environment or handles food already in his possession.
22   Takes or manipulates food. More complex manipulation of food (such as with utensil rather than with fingers).
23   Transports food. The subject moves food from one part of the environment to another.
24   Disorganizes with food. Subject smears, messes, or throws food.

Manual Activities (25–29). Actions of the subject upon some type of item (toy, clothing, etc.).

25   Transfers item. The subject transfers an item from himself to another person or locus.
26   Takes or handles item. Subject takes an item from a spot in the environment, or carries out a single manipulation with an item.
27   Manipulates item. More complex and difficult item manipulations such as building with blocks, stringing beads, pushing small cars, working a puzzle.
28   Transports item. Moving an article from one place to another in the environment.
29   Throws or rolls item. Purposive, usually interactive, throwing or rolling of appropriate play materials.

Negative Reinforcement (30–38). This area encompasses behaviors best described as disrupting the emitted behavior of another person or group.

30   Withholds sanction. Subject protests, denies, or challenges a statement made to him, or refuses to carry out a requested act.
31   Shows discomfort. By behavior or verbalizations, the subject evidences fatigue, tension, fear, or pain.

32 Expresses displeasure. Subject emits an expression of unhappiness.

33 Criticizes or derogates. Subject is critical, derogatory, accusatory, belligerent, or thoughtless.

34 Expresses hostility. Subject gives an extreme statement of dislike or disapproval.

35 Interferes or restricts. Subject physically interferes with actions of another person.

36 Resists or rejects. Subject reacts to perceived interference with resistance.

37 Threatens or frightens. Subject gesturally or verbally threatens another person with censure, loss of privilege, or punishment.

38 Assaults. Physical action which involves any assault by one person upon the corpus of another person or object.

Positive Reinforcement (40–48). Each of these predicates is essentially a counterpart of one in the previous decile. All the categories refer to behavior which supports the ongoing behavior of another person or expresses a state of satisfaction with the self.

40 Permits or sanctions. Subject authorizes some proposed behavior.

41 Expresses solicitude. Subject expresses concern for well-being or comfort or contentment of another person.

42 Expresses pleasure. Subject emits signs of positive affect expression.

43 Approves, encourages. Subject enhances the self-esteem of person to whom the response is directed.

44 Expresses affection. Subject gives physical or verbal indications of love and affection.

45 Facilitates. Subject provides physical help to another person.

46 Excuses. Subject emits a response which rationalizes or defends another person's behavior.

47 Bargains, promises. Subject makes some kind of desired reinforcement contingent upon a particular type of response emission.

48 Protects, defends. Subject takes anticipatory action to defend the person or rights of another individual or item.

Body Activities (50–59). Actions in which some type or quality of body activity is the primary feature of the response.

50 Increases or accelerates. Clear acceleration of the speed or tempo at which a response is emitted.

51 Decreases or retards. An inhibition, diminution, or cessation of body activities.

52 Perioralizes. An awkward neologism necessary to get non-nutritive

oral activities into verb form — that is, sucks thumb, bites nails, chews gum, and so forth.

53   Acts in situ. This category encompasses most non-locomotory body activities except those involved in eating or perioralizing or in the manipulation of play materials.

54   Adjusts or accommodates. Action which refines a body or manual activity.

55   Kinesthetizes. Any sort of body manipulation that primarily involves stimulation of kinesthetic receptors.

56   Locomotes. All categories of movement in space in which the subject propels himself without vehicular support.

57   LMA's. This is a local shorthand for "engages in large muscle activities."

58   Rhythmicizes. Acts involving rhythmic activities such as marching, dancing, or swaying.

59   Voids or excretes. All preparatory responses as well as the consummatory responses of voiding or excreting.

Miscellaneous (60–66). This area covers a number of unrelated miscellaneous items that either did not belong in any of the other areas or could not be contained within the number of digits (usually ten) assigned to a given area.

60   Acts or happens. This predicate refers to virtually any type of behavior or environmental event which does not fit one of the other categories. Most characteristically, it refers to some salient stimulus event produced by a nonhuman object to which an observed subject responds, as when a toy crashes to the floor and elicits a look from a subject.

61   Caretakes. Any action that serves the function of keeping people or objects clean and orderly.

62   Consummates activity. This is a verb in the language which has two meanings. It refers to the completion of a task (a type of request often received by a child) or else to the successful consummation of a somewhat prolonged series of goal-related activities. The second usage is optional.

63   Fails. This verb is the counterpart of the second meaning of 62 above. It is used at the end of a series of continued goal-directed activities which culminate in failure.

64   Disorganizes. This is a largely qualitative category describing generally disruptive or explosive activities.

65   Disintegrates emotionally. Wild social or physical behavior such as one sees in temper tantrums or in prolonged indiscriminate assaultive episodes.

66   Makes music (or sound patterns). The production of music by items of equipment (record player) or persons.

Control Techniques (70–74). This category covers suggestions or mandates for specific responses from another person or attempts to influence another's behavior by offering to carry out a presumably desired form of behavior. Designation of these responses as control techniques does not imply that many other predicates in the system are not also intended as techniques of behavior control. This is especially true of the predicates within the categories of negative and positive reinforcement and of several of those in the information processing area. The main difference is that the intent of behaviors coded into many of the other categories is to influence future response by providing appropriate reinforcement or informational feedback, whereas the intent of those designated as control techniques is to influence and modify ongoing behavior. Coding of these predicates is rather complicated, and any interested person should read carefully the section of the APPROACH manual devoted to these responses. Briefly, the technique involves one statement which reports that a control statement has been emitted and defines the type (positive, negative, or contingent offer), a second which tells what has been requested or offered (and thus that does not refer to emitted behavior), and at least one subsequent statement reporting the fate of the request.

70   Suggests. An implied request delivered in the form of a declarative or interrogative rather than an imperative.
71   Requests. Clear requests for specific action on the part of the person to whom the request was addressed.
72   Inhibits. This is identical to 70 above, except that the suggestion is for inhibition or cessation of a particular type of activity.
73   Forbids. A firm command that a certain act be terminated.
74   Offers. A clear offer on the part of the subject to carry out some particular act for or with the person to whom the offer is made.

At present there are some sixty-five verbs in the APPROACH language — a limited action vocabulary, to be sure. This means that thirty-four predicates can be added without the assignment of another column to the five-digit numerical statement. By setting up the model so that it could be "open" rather than "closed," the authors hoped to produce a flexible methodological tool which would have relevance to a broad range of research problems. The option to add (or delete) specific verbs contributes significantly to that flexibility.

Object of the Behavioral Clause. The objects which can be coded are the same as the subjects; therefore, it is not necessary to repeat the definitions and the numerical assignments. The fourth column of the five-column statement indicates the object of the clause.

Qualifiers of the Action. The last touch of literary elegance permitted in the dry numerical language of the APPROACH system is in the form of a limited number of qualifiers of the action. The qualifiers included have been carefully screened and reflect personal research preoccupations. It is conceivable that for many investigations needing naturalistic observational data, the information in this part of the clause would be redundant. If such were the case, one would simply eliminate the fifth digit and code only four digits. Similarly, for other research questions, a completely different set of qualifiers might be needed and could easily be substituted. The adverbial information is important for many of the questions for which the coding system was designed, and the qualifiers currently assigned digits in the fifth column thus merit brief description.

0   Ineptly. The behavior was emitted ineptly, incorrectly, or clumsily.

1   Verbally. The emitted behavior was accompanied by a verbalization. Some verbs (e.g., converses, questions, explains, etc.) require verbalization, in which case the appearance of a 1 in the fifth column is redundant (but is nonetheless used for the sake of consistency). Others, however, may be emitted either silently or verbally (e.g., a person may establish contact with a wave or with a spoken greeting), and for our present research purposes it was important to distinguish between these two types of action.

2   Involving interpersonal physical contact. The action involved tactile contact between two people.

3   Intensely. The action was carried out with vigor, vehemence, or intensity.

4   In a specified manner, place, or time. This is an extremely informative qualifier, generally related to control statements, implying that not just any type of action would be acceptable within a particular category but that a rigorously defined type was expected or occurred.

5   In a manner, place, or time other than that specified. Action carried out disregarded some explicit (request) or implicit (rule) behavioral sanction.

6   Imitatively. An act was emitted in direct imitation of a similar response emitted by another person.

7   In continuation. Although APPROACH uses behavior units rather than time units, some device was necessary to equalize the contribu-

tion made to the behavior record of actions that occupied very brief time spans and those that lasted longer. Accordingly, if the behavior of the CF continues without change for more than five seconds, the same behavior statement is repeated with a 7 in the fifth column (regardless of what digit was there before) to indicate that this is a continuation of the behavior which was going on during the previous statement and not a new episode involving the same predicate.

8   Complexly. This qualifier permits two statements to be joined together to indicate that two types of behavior occurred simultaneously. It appears in the fifth column of the second part of the statement.

9   No information. Many behavioral statements need no qualifier and end with the numeral 9 in order to simplify computer programing by having all statements use the same number of digits.

BEHAVIOR SETTINGS

In order for any behavioral coding system to be useful for ecological analysis, it must report significant aspects of the behavioral setting as faithfully as it reports emitted behaviors. As in the case with behavior units, setting units may be described along a continuum ranging from macroscopic to microscopic. For some research purposes, perhaps only the grossest description of setting would be sufficient, as, for instance, home, school, playground, and so forth. For other purposes, a much more finely grained analysis of the setting might be necessary — that is, home with father present and home with father absent.

The setting codes currently used in APPROACH are probably much more provincial than the behavior codes. That is, they are not only limited to the fairly narrow world of the nursery school and the home of the young child, but they occasionally refer to a research procedure limited to the Children's Center project at Syracuse University. Therefore, the exact numerical codes will not be presented; rather, the types of information contained in the five columns will merely be defined and examples given. Persons needing more detail may refer to the APPROACH manual (Caldwell et al., 1967).

Setting Alert. An announcement that information about setting is being given occurs in the form of five-digit statement beginning with 9. It is to be expected that the setting will change several times in a record, and each statement beginning with 9 defines certain characteristics of the new setting.

Activity Identification. This information pertains to the general type of activity taking place in the environment in which the observation is being made. In the present code it covers such activities as lunch or snack, nap, toileting, free play, structured learning time, story period, music period, art period, gym or outdoor play, transition periods, medical or psychological examination, assembly or party, field trips. This is reported in the second and third columns of the five-digit setting statement.

Geographic Region. This information, contained in the fourth column of a setting statement, identifies the region in which the behavior is emitted. Regions assigned numbers in the present formulation are school, home, laboratory or examining room, special teaching area, or other geographic region.

Social Setting. The fifth column of the setting statement reports on the people other than the Central Figure present during the observation. At present, it permits such interactants as the following to be identified: mother, father, mother plus father, one other child, more than one other child, a nonfamily adult, nonfamily adult or adults and child or children, one or both parents plus another adult with or without other children, child alone, or other social pattern.

RELIABILITY

With every step back from the live behavior of the subject, there is a certain loss of information. That is, there is undoubtedly a loss when someone tries to describe what is taking place in the fast-moving behavioral world of the young child, and there is a further loss when someone takes the written description and converts it into a set of symbols suitable for statistical analysis. Although information about both types of reliability is necessary for an evaluation of a particular method, the first type of loss (inter-observer unreliability) is often, for practical reasons, difficult to estimate. However, since the training of observers is a vital first step in the conduct of an observational study, and since the presence of the observer has minimal impact on the subjects in our setting, we investigated inter-observer reliability as a first step. This was done by stationing two observers in the same environmental field, with one never coming close enough to the other to hear what was being whispered by the second person, and having each make a standard observation. One of the two observers then coded both protocols. Inter-coder reliability was computed in the standard way of having two coders code the same record.

Agreement between the resultant protocols was computed according to the formula $A = (U - D_c)/(U + \frac{1}{2}X)$, in which U represents the total number of units mutually designated by both coders (or by the same coder working from two protocols referring to the same behavior), D_c represents the number of mutually coded clauses in which coders differed in their coding of the column (or columns) for which reliability is being computed, and X represents the number of clauses coded by one person but not by the other. A less stringent test of agreement is obtained by ignoring the extra clauses coded by one observer and comparing agreement on only those units coded by both persons — that is, $A = (U - D_c)/U$.

Percentages of Inter-observer Agreement
for APPROACH Records

Part of Statement	Agreement	Agreement without "Extra" Codes [a]
Inter-observer Agreement		
Subject	65 [b]	99 [c]
Predicate	55 [b]	85 [c]
Object	53 [b]	82 [c]
Qualifier	58 [b]	85 [c]
Total statement	42 [b]	64 [c]
Inter-coder Agreement		
Subject	87 [d]	99 [e]
Predicate	76 [d]	86 [e]
Object	70 [d]	82 [e]
Qualifier	70 [d]	82 [e]
Total statement	52 [d]	60 [e]

[a] "Extra" codes are those assigned by one coder but not by the other.

[b] Based on two simultaneously obtained protocols assigned a total of 391 units.

[c] Based on the 255 common units coded in both protocols.

[d] Based on seven pairs of protocols assigned a total of 2,-981 units.

[e] Based on the 2,625 common units designated by both coders and ignoring the 356 units designated by one coder but not by the other.

Inter-observer reliability of both types is reported in the upper half of the table above. It is apparent that the slight differences in wording used by the two observers led to different unitizing, in that the reliabilities based upon coding of actions inferred from both protocols are respectably high. Thus, when one ignores the number of times the coder reported a behavioral clause when reading one protocol but not when working from another protocol presumably describing the same behavioral episode, there is agreement on the designation of subject of the clause in 99 per cent of the units. However, when one takes into consideration the disagreement implied in the designation of any person or object as subject of the clause on the basis of one protocol and the absence of any comparable designation on the basis of the other protocol, the agreement drops by 34 percentage points. Similar drops (around 30 percentage points) are observed for the predicates, the objects, and the qualifiers, with a drop of 22 percentage points observed when all digits are considered simultaneously. These data on inter-observer reliability highlight the necessity for considering the sensitivity and reliability of the persons who report observational data. On the basis of what we know about the APPROACH, and from a scanning of the individual protocols which yielded these figures, it is apparent that slight differences in wording may lead to the designation of different codes, and a different total number of codes, for the same behavior. Training in this kind of reliability task is now standard for all persons who obtain protocols and code the records.

In the lower half of the table can be seen data on inter-coder reliability based on seven protocols coded by random pairing of three coders. As is obvious, we are apparently better at coding than we are at observing and reporting. That is, even taking into account the differences in units assigned by the different coders, the level of agreement for all parts of the statement combined was 52 per cent. This is quite high, considering the fact that for any given behavioral clause there are over forty thousand possible numerical statements available to the coder. Again, as in inter-observer reliability, the problem of unitizing is apparent. When one disregards the "extra" codes (those assigned by one coder but not by the other), agreement for the subject of the behavioral clause is almost perfect and that for the predicates is about as high as one ever obtains in such a task. Thus it appears that obtaining reliability is not a major obstacle to further development of APPROACH as an observation system for studies in the field of behavioral ecology.

Data Yielded by the Technique

INDIVIDUAL PROFILES

To illustrate the type of data which can be extracted via the APPROACH technique, records of five children were chosen. These children were all in attendance at a special day care center operated by my colleagues and me. There are five separate classrooms in the program, one each for young infants, toddlers, two's, three's, and four's. For this analysis a half-hour observation was made on one child from each group during a semi-structured classroom period. Figures 1–5 represent actual number of responses coded for each child (all behavioral clauses with 0 as subject) and the number of responses received by the child from other individuals (i.e., all behavioral clauses with 2, 3, 5, or 8 as subject and 0 as object). This distinction is important to keep in mind, since one should not infer that the teachers and nurses did not carry out other actions than those directed toward the central figure of the observation. It will be remembered that, unless a teacher is the central figure of the observation, only those teacher behaviors which are directed toward or emitted in the immediate vicinity of the central figure will be reported. Thus, the behavioral mosaic of the child is considerably more complete than that of the adult. Similarly, it should be kept in mind that the type of code used for the current APPROACH protocols collapses across all individuals of a given classification except for the central figure. Hence, all female adults from whom the central figure receives any response will be coded 2 as the subject of the behavioral clause and will thus be indistinguishable from one another. The same thing is true of male adults, female children, and male children. Only the central figure stands out as a complete individual; all other actors are coded by category.

For this presentation the behavioral predicates are grouped into the larger categories of response represented by the individual actions. For example, all of the subcategories classified as Information Processing (confirms, shows, converses, etc.), all those considered patterns of Negative Responses (withholds sanction, shows tension, shows displeasure, etc.), and other within-decile predicates are grouped together.

The behavior profile of Juanita, a nine-month-old girl, reflects clearly the restriction in range of behaviors possible for a nonmotile, nonverbal infant. Her modal response was "attending," with an adult receiving most of the attention and the remainder divided between another child and a group of children. But more than thirty times the little girl did not respond to (ignored) stimuli considered by the observer to be salient enough to elicit a response. The other major categories of infant behavior were manual activities (manipulating objects, transferring objects to and from the environment) and body activities (non-locomotory and locomotory actions). There were a few episodes of negative emotional response, the majority of which can be recognized as representing whimpers or other signs

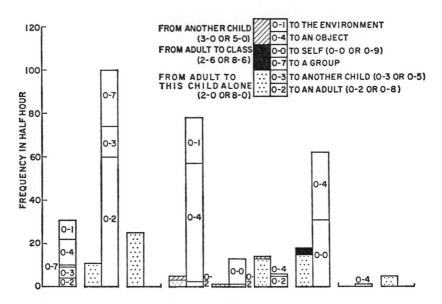

Figure 1. Behaviors emitted by a 9-month-old girl and received from adults in a day care center — one half-hour observation.

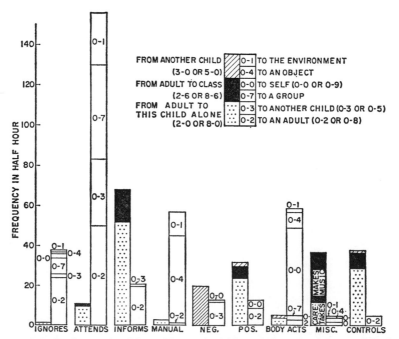

Figure 2. Behaviors emitted by a 23-month-old boy and received from adults in a day care center — one half-hour observation.

94

of distress directed toward no one in particular (identified on the graph as emitted to the self). Likewise there were a few smiles, most of which were directed at one of the adults in the environment. The baby did little else.

Perhaps somewhat surprising is the paucity of adult responses directed toward this child. The most characteristic response was some type of information processing, with body actions, some smiles or words of approval or praise directed to the baby, a little bit of attention, and a few control statements essentially representing the remainder of the adult activities. Quite obviously, these would be influenced by the time of day (only at meal or snack time would one get food behavior, and caretaking behavior would be influenced by time of day), but even so, the range and frequency of adult behaviors appeared to be smaller than one might have expected.

Figure 2 presents the array for Andy, a boy of almost two who had been in the toddler group for about a year. On first glance he appears again to be largely an "attender," proportionately less likely to engage in manual or body activities than the baby and just about as prone not to respond to super-threshold stimulation. His attention is divided almost equally among the adults, the other children (singly or in a group), and the physical environment. If he ignores a stimulus, he appears relatively more likely to ignore an adult. In this record, the bonus associated with being in a group becomes apparent. With the infant, all but two adult responses were directed toward the one child as an individual; thus what the child received was relatively more expensive in terms of available teacher time. With the toddler, however, about one fourth of the information processing, the positive reinforcement, and the control techniques were emitted to the child as part of the total group rather than to him as a single individual; in "making music" the teacher obviously performed for the whole group. The APPROACH thus very effectively separates those encounters with the environment that are directed to the child by himself and those in which he is one of several recipients toward whom a particular pattern of stimulation is directed. It is entirely conceivable that these two types of input (detected by a difference in the fourth column of the numerical statement) produce different probabilities of response in the child, and that these probabilities differ as a function of age of the child. This is empirically testable, and the answers have great relevance for the planning of educational programs for young children.

Figure 3 presents the protocol of a two-year-old girl, Frankie. For the first time, responses primarily involving the distance receptors (attend-

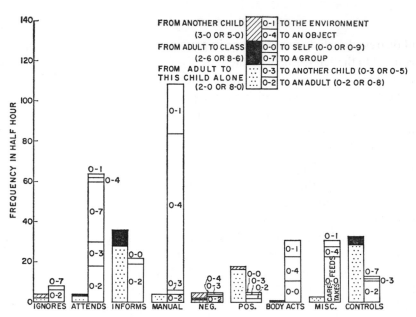

Figure 3. Behaviors emitted by a 2-year-old girl and received from adults in a day care center — one half-hour observation.

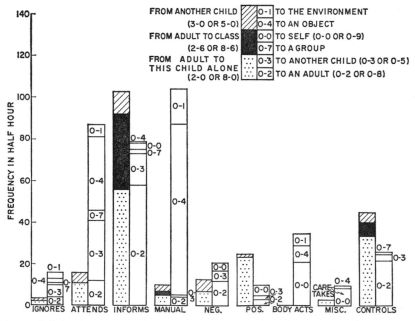

Figure 4. Behaviors emitted by a 3-year-old boy and received from adults in a day care center — one half-hour observation.

ing) are not the most frequent; instead, the manipulation of objects becomes the modal response. Withholding attention from salient stimuli occurs very infrequently in this record. The relative infrequency of body activities makes one suspect limitations imposed by the setting, although this
could represent a salient individual response mode. The rise of information processing (almost all directed to an adult) and of the emitting of
control statements points to the increased acquisition of verbal ability. On
the receiving end, Frankie received more information than anything else
from the adults in her environment and essentially nothing from the other
children. Following information processing in frequency were control
statements, with most of these directed to the child as an individual. The
only other adult response that occurred with any frequency was positive
reinforcement; even so, it did not occur with so high a frequency as one
would expect in such a special environment. This observation again illustrates some of the versatility of the technique and its usefulness for testing
specific hypotheses — such as, When in a given session a child receives
more control statements than positive reinforcements, does he engage in
more negative and disorganized behaviors than when the proportion is reversed?

In Figure 4 we have the behavior profile of a three-year-old boy, Merritt. This child's looking and listening ("attends") rises back to the level
observed in the younger children, and he is also heavily engaged in object
manipulation. But in this record we get a picture for the first time of a verbal child busily engaged in information transfer. Also noticeable is the fact
that in the observation period he emits more negative than positive behaviors, that he occasionally ignores stimuli directed toward him, and that he
engages in quite a bit of behavior designed to control his teachers. In this
record one recognizes for the first time the impact of the other children in
the group. Sizable amounts of attention and information processing go to
another child or to a group of children. On the receiving side, almost half
of the information processing comes to him either by virtue of the fact that
he is present in a group or else comes from one of the other children. Half
of the negative encounters and a small number of control statements come
from other children in the group. It is interesting to note that Merritt
emitted more negative than positive behaviors but that his proportion was
reversed in terms of behaviors received from other people in the environment.

Figure 5 presents a profile of a four-year-old girl, Laurel, in the oldest group of children in attendance at the Center. A quick glance indicates that this is a watching and a talking child but that her talking is self-oriented rather than communication-oriented. She divides her watching almost equally among the adults, the children, and the environment. The fact that she spends half of her information processing time talking to herself clearly indicates that she is somewhat withdrawn from the group activities. This conclusion is further substantiated by the fact that she is not infrequently ignored by both the adults and the children in the classroom, that she receives very little information from either adults or children during the session, that she has many more negative than positive encounters with other children — although fortunately this is reversed with adults, as is shown very clearly in the small number of control statements received by Laurel from adults. If it were not for the fact that she spends so much of her time talking to herself, one might simply infer that the teachers in the classroom were satisfied with what she was doing; however, the total pattern suggests more that the child was pretty much left alone. Nobody bothered to tell her to do something. In this case, the experience of being in a group was prob-

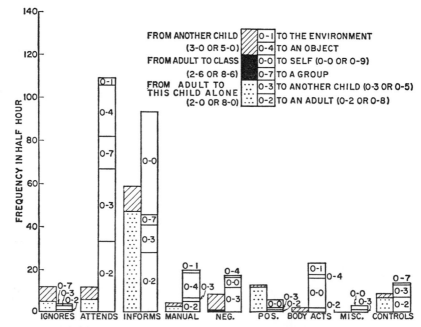

Figure 5. Behaviors emitted by a 4-year-old girl and received from adults in a day care center — one half-hour observation.

ably subtractive rather than additive in terms of total amount of stimulation received.

These five protocols were selected randomly from the age groups represented (they were the first records coded and checked). Obviously, records in the different age groups will need to be combined before a smooth picture of the developmental sequences of behavior can be extracted. But the APPROACH technique is intended less for normative than for idiographic study, and it is perhaps best suited for research questions concerned with the relation between specific types of interpersonal or physical stimuli and specific types of response. For such questions, the analysis of individual records, even if summed and grouped into patterns, will always be necessary.

After this introduction to the arrays of emitted and received behaviors in the environments of the five children in the different age groups, the incidence of certain types of behavior in all five environments will be examined. Figure 6 presents a graphic summary of the proportion of time spent in the different categories of behavioral predicates by the five children. Here the responses have been converted from the absolute number of clauses involving different predicates to percentages in order to facilitate comparison. The number of absolute responses appears to be correlated more with life style than with age. In these five children, for example, the numbers of codes in the order of ascending age are 288, 367, 288, 388, and 290. For all five children, looking and listening (attending) represent a major portion of their activities, with this being especially true for the two youngest. Next in magnitude is the broad category of object manipulation. The very low incidence of this response in the oldest girl makes one suspect either an atypical situation or a somewhat atypical child, for there is little doubt that the nursery school world involves a great deal of object manipulation. Body activities, at least in this semi-structured setting (an indoor period involving some cognitive or artistic activities) diminish with age. Information processing by the child increases with age, and so does the tendency to attempt to control the behavior of others. The incidence of positive behaviors remains fairly constant across all five children, with negative behaviors dropping and then increasing again.

For each of the major categories of predicates, a chi square was computed using a k-by-2 model. That is, the frequency with which each child emitted a response in one category (ignored, attended, informed, etc.) was tallied in contrast to the number of responses emitted in any other

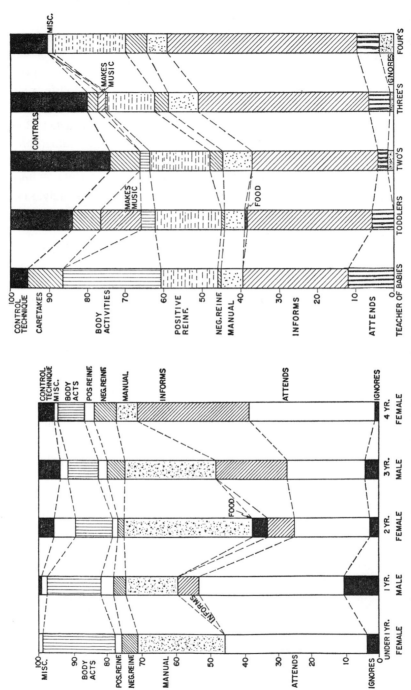

Figure 6. Percentage of time spent by five children in different categories of behavioral predicates. *Figure 7.* Percentage of time spent by adults in the environments of five children in different categories of behavioral predicates.

100

category. Such an analysis is justifiable only as a means of comparing samples of events in a population of possible events and should not be interpreted as referring to a distribution of children representative of different age groups. The true N for each sample of events is still only one person. For the data of Figure 6 all of the chi squares except those for negative and positive reinforcement were significant at or beyond the .01 level. Thus, we could conclude that the predicates were not randomly distributed among the five children.

TEACHER BEHAVIOR

Although each observation is centered on one particular child, a great deal is revealed about teacher behavior in the classrooms. In each instance the "teacher" is actually a composite of all the teachers who might have interacted with the observed child. This type of analysis thus characterizes teacher behavior from a child's-eye view.

Figure 7 summarizes the prototypical teacher behavior emitted to each of the five children. There was considerable variability in the number of absolute child-directed teacher behaviors, with the youngest to oldest figures being 109, 250, 141, 214, and 130, respectively. When these are converted to percentages, however, it can be seen that there is a fairly high degree of consistency in the composite teacher behavior directed to the five children. Information processing increases with age; body activities and caretaking decline with age; and control techniques vary significantly, apparently reflecting differences in the children's behavior. The proportions of teacher-emitted attention, manual activities, negative reinforcement, and positive reinforcement do not differ from child to child. Thus, one would conclude that the behavior of trained teachers tends, except where age-specific needs dictate that certain kinds of teacher behavior must occur (such as the high incidence of caretaking in the three younger groups), to remain somewhat more constant from child to child than do comparable patterns of child-emitted behavior.

Verbal and Nonverbal Behavior. But that teacher response, even in an area to which much training in the Children's Center program is directed, is not totally independent of the pattern of child response is demonstrated in Figure 8, which collapses across predicates in the APPROACH language and attends only to the proportion of predicates emitted with or without a verbal component. (It will be remembered that this information is supplied in the fifth digit of the numerical code.) As would be expected, there is a clear increase in the number of predicates emitted verbally. The increase is not perfectly ordinal, however, reaching a peak in these children with the three-year-old boy and then declining somewhat for the four-year-old girl (obviously an individual and not a normative reversal). The relation between tendency for the child to behave verbally and age is highly significant ($\chi^2 = 176$, $p < .001$). But verbal-nonverbal teacher behavior is not randomly distributed either ($\chi^2 = 22$, $p < .01$), a fact which perhaps surprised the teachers in the Children's Center program more than it will anyone else. As mentioned before, they are trained not only to respond to all the vocalizations of the children with some verbal response but also to do a great deal of labeling of objects and events in the environment and to interpret experiences verbally as a means of stimulating language learning. But the fact stands out sharply that it is perhaps simply more difficult to talk to someone who does not talk to you. There is a rank difference correlation of .90 between the proportions of child and adult behaviors that occur verbally.

Types of Information Processing. Thus far, all the data presented for the five children who served as subjects for the material reported here have been in gross categories — that is, all the different types of information processing have been lumped together, all types of object manipulation, and so forth. If these categories are sufficient, then one might justifiably wonder why the APPROACH language includes so many highly specific verbs. The answer is that they are there because frequently one wants to know exactly how a person processes information, dispenses positive reinforcement, or tries to control someone else's behavior. This is simple to accomplish with APPROACH, and those of us who have worked on the technique like to use the metaphor of switching to a different lens with a higher level of magnification.

In Figure 9 is magnified a category in which all persons concerned with the process of education are vitally interested — techniques of transmitting information from one person to another. For this presentation we have chosen to use the actual number of responses within the information processing category rather than percentages, as the impact of any given type may vary as a function of the total amount. Figure 9 shows that the infant not only received less information in general but also fewer types; only the categories show, converse, and teach appeared with any significant frequency during her half hour. The three-year-old received the largest amount of information transfer. Although the four-year-old received less,

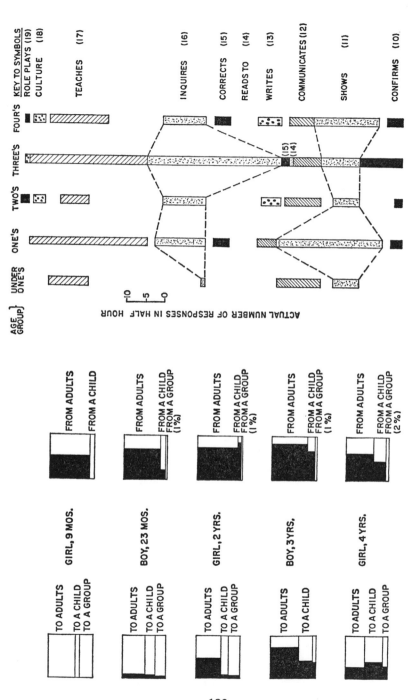

Figure 8. Percentage of verbal and nonverbal behaviors emitted and received by five children. *Figure 9.* Methods of information processing used by teachers with five children of different ages.

103

she received some via all 10 predicates contained in the APPROACH. The significantly high use of questions by the teachers with the three-year-old appears interesting in relation to the supposed capacity of a question to make a child think.

The four categories of information processing—shows, converses, inquires, and teaches—found in the records of all five children were submitted to a chi square analysis. The resulting figure of 48.98 ($p<.01$) indicates that these types of information processing were not randomly employed by the teachers and randomly distributed among the five children. Further work on the relation between type of information processing received from the teachers and type of cognitive output variables in the children is currently in process.

Control Techniques. The world of the small child is generally filled with directives and prohibitions. Although they supply an important teaching function, such control techniques almost invariably interfere to some extent with a child's ongoing behavior and thus can frequently be expected to encounter some resistance. Our parent education literature is filled with suggestions about ways of making this control process more palatable for the young child—for example, make a suggestion rather than a peremptory command and avoid negatives if possible. Since we were interested in knowing whether such specific variants on the theme of "Do as I tell you" actually have different effects, five different control verbs were accepted in the APPROACH language. They might be thought of as ranging along a continuum from permitting a wide range of acceptable responses to permitting essentially no variability. As defined earlier in the chapter, they are: offers, suggests, commands, inhibits, and forbids. As a first step in understanding the control world of the young child, we examined the types of control statements emitted by the adults and each of the five children. These data are presented in Figure 10.

The youngest child receives few control statements, and these are all of the gentle suggestion type; the baby emits none at all. (This should not be interpreted as meaning that the infant does not attempt to control other people in her environment. Obviously the child who cries and looks at an adult may be seeking to effect some change in the adult's response. By and large, we have coded conservatively and have simply regarded this as an expression of negative emotion. However, the infant who holds up his hands to an adult is coded as making a nonverbal request.) The toddler receives the largest number of control statements, as would be predicted,

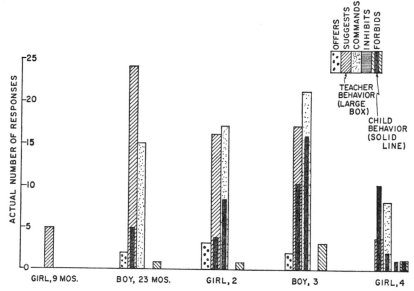

Figure 10. Control techniques used by teachers with five children of different ages.

and in his environment they were primarily of the indirect type. He emitted only indirect control messages, and the chances are that they were of the nonverbal type described above. The two-year-old girl receives more direct than indirect control statements, and her pattern of attempting to control mirrors that of the adult. Exactly the same relation is observed in the three-year-old boy. The four-year-old girl, who was shown on her individual profile to be fairly withdrawn from social interaction with both adults and children, reverses the pattern of control statements that she receives. Whereas she receives more direct ones, her own repertoire involves more of the hesitant, not-certain-of-success, indirect type. In contrast to the other children, however, she is willing to try the negative variety of control. All adults use the negative control statements very sparingly. They show the effects of their training.

The data for Figure 10 were subjected to a chi square analysis similar to those carried out for the other arrays of behavior. As negative control statements were so infrequently used, they were ignored. A 2-by-5 chi square comparing the incidence of "suggests" and "commands" in the behavioral fields of the five children yielded a figure of 17.38, significant at the .01 level. This indicates a non-random use of the indirect-direct dimension with the different children, with teachers of the very young preferring the indirect mode of control technique.

Discussion

No facts exist apart from the methods by which they are obtained, and the "facts" of early child development have seldom been obtained by direct observation in minimally contrived settings. Each time a new method or approach to the study of human behavior is introduced, a new world of facts emerges. Few facts about mental development were available before the introduction of the intelligence test, and once the methods were introduced, the facts fairly flew into the literature. Such facts remain until new methods prove them false. Similarly, the facts about personality study that were obtained when the chief method of study was the self-administered questionnaire and the "new facts" that emerged when projective techniques were introduced in many respects bore little resemblance to one another. Undoubtedly, in any scientific field there is a reciprocal process involved in the development of new methodologies and the acquisition of new facts.

The APPROACH technique is not a new method; people have been observing other people for a long time. But it is a new way of compiling and organizing information gathered via observation, and as such, it offers the possibility of bringing new facts into the literature of child development. It is impossible not to feel a bit presumptuous in introducing a new technique to a scientific audience, since the simple introduction seems to imply an invitation to accept it, to try it, to endorse it. Whether such an invitation is implicit in my decision to respond to the honor of the Minnesota invitation by talking about this new technique which has grown out of our research program rather than by presenting other data from the research will have to be interpreted by the audience. Actually, my experience with other behavioral scientists confirms the fact that they are quite an independent breed, often preferring to develop their own methods rather than use those that have been developed by others. But, as mentioned earlier, a tremendous amount of time has already gone into the development of this procedure, with significant amounts of continuing research time committed to the task of refining the system, improving both observer and coder reliability, rooting out ambiguities, training new people to use the technique, and so forth. And although within our own research framework, we fully expect the yield of significant data about human behavior to liquidate this tremendous debt of time and energy, perhaps we cannot help but feel that it would be nice to have some assistance in achieving the payoff.

At this time there is a generally heightened interest in observational methods, particularly among people doing research on intervention in early childhood. Dissatisfaction with standard techniques of assessment is high, and there appears to be a general consensus that better observational techniques — or rather, better techniques for using data based on naturalistic observation — will help to provide more meaningful descriptions of baseline performance for children and more representative samples on the basis of which one can infer areas in which improvement occurs or fails to occur. But perhaps even more pressing is the need for a technique which accurately describes the environment in which learning occurs (Caldwell, 1967). It is easy to be seduced by labels, to assume that any environment which calls itself an enrichment program does indeed offer enrichment to the children enrolled. Similarly, in view of the new interest in comparative educational research at the early childhood level, some technique which can accurately describe and characterize different environments is sorely needed. It is our conviction that the APPROACH is uniquely suited to such endeavors and that it can do a better job of characterizing different learning environments than such labels as "traditional," "Montessori," "Social reinforcement."

For half a decade now I have been deeply immersed in research relating to the early learning process in children who have been labeled "disadvantaged." There appears little doubt that such a label is appropriate when one evaluates the children during the late preschool or early elementary years and at essentially any time point thereafter. But, at the same time, components of the environment which are presumably "disadvantaging" have been largely inferred rather than observed. Certainly this is true of the very early period, during which the environment apparently retreats from even an approximation of adequacy to patent insufficiency to prime further cognitive growth. During the course of this research I have become convinced of the necessity for more ecological studies of the disadvantaged infant and young child in a variety of environments. Only when we have more data of this sort available shall we be able to pinpoint the kinds of environmental input associated with the type of development desired by parents and valued by society. It is our conviction that the APPROACH technique offers a useful and potentially productive technique for obtaining such data.

Summary

This paper has introduced a new APPROACH to ecological studies of human behavior which will, we hope, prove a useful tool for behavioral scientists. The technique involves breaking up ongoing behavior into a series of grammatical clauses, each of which describes a relatively discrete act. Elements of the APPROACH language report the subject of the behavioral clause, the predicate, the object (if there is one), and refine the clause with a few selected modifiers of the verb which permit some qualitative descriptions to creep into a language which is really quite monotonous and limited — it is not at all mellifluous, has only nine subjects and objects, and only some sixty to ninety verbs. It is, however, an easily learned foreign language which is responded to with great enthusiasm by the behavioral scientist's principal foreign-language-speaking ally, the electronic computer. The aim of the method is to permit careful study of social behavior in a completely non-artificial situation. Through this technique we hope to begin to understand better the relation between setting and behavior and to improve our understanding of sequences of behavior. The technique appears to work equally well in monadic, diadic, or polyadic situations.

Kurt Koffka once said that if one looked only through a microscope, one would never know what a face looked like. This is undoubtedly true, and faces are rather nice to look at. But without the microscope we should never have learned what bacteria and cells looked like, and how they acted and interacted. The APPROACH technique is rather like a somewhat crude microscope for behavioral analysis. Perhaps from the method we shall never learn what a child or a mother or a teacher *looks like* (though of course we have cameras for that), but it is our hope that it will help us understand more fully how the behavior of one person is related to what that person has done before and to what the people and objects in his environment make available as a behavioral milieu. And if that happens, AP-PROACH will have arrived.

References

Barker, R. G., & H. F. Wright. Psychological ecology and the problem of psychosocial development. *Child Development*, 1949, 20, 131–143.

————. *Midwest and its children: The psychological ecology of an American town.* Evanston, Ill.: Row, Peterson, 1954.

Bishop, B. M. Mother-child interaction and the social behavior of children. *Psychological Monographs*, 1951, 65, No. 2, 1–34.

Caldwell, B. M. Descriptive evaluations of development and of developmental settings. *Pediatrics*, 1967, 40, 46–54.

————, A. S. Honig, & R. Wynn. APPROACH — A procedure for patterning responses of adults and children. Unpublished MS., 1967.

Darwin, C. A biographical sketch of an infant. *Mind*, 1877, 11, 286–294.

Flanders, N. A. Teacher influence, pupil attitude, and achievement. U.S. Department of Health, Education, and Welfare, Office of Education, Cooperative Research Monograph No. 12. Washington, D.C.: Government Printing Office, 1965. 126 pp.

Gewirtz, J. L., & H. Gewirtz. Stimulus conditions, infant behavior, and social learning in different child rearing environments. Observation Manual. Unpublished MS., 1962.

Preyer, W. *Mind of the child*, trans. H. W. Brown. New York: Appleton, 1888–1889.

Sears, R. R. A theoretical framework for personality and social behavior. *American Psychologist*, 1951, 6, 476–483.

Wright, H. F. Observational child study, in P. H. Mussen, ed., *Handbook of research methods in child development*, pp. 71–139. New York: Wiley, 1960.

◈ MAURICE HERSHENSON ◈

Effects of Cognition on Perception: A Problem and a Paradigm for Developmental Study

THE broad aim of this paper is to bring to attention an underdeveloped area of the study of development, namely, the changes in perception which should — perhaps must — accompany cognitive development. Certainly, the study of cognitive development has flowered, and, just as certainly, its fruition carries implications for perceptual development.

Indeed, perceptual-cognitive development has received some attention, but this has focused primarily on infancy. Perhaps because perceptual structure "ought" to precede cognitive structure or perhaps because visually guided responses, which are clearly involving the perceptual system, dominate early life — for whatever reason, early "cognitive" development has generally been seen to be perceptual. But this development does not reflect the action of cognition *on* perception as much as events which occur at a stage when perception and cognition are synonymous. The class of effects which require study are modifications of the perceptual system that accompany later changes in cognitive structure.

An example might clarify the attributes of the class: The "wife and mother-in-law" figure provides a constant stimulus which may be "restructured" in perception. One sees an old or a young lady depending upon the original description of the figure; both faces can be perceived upon the viewer's being told that they are in the figure. This is an effect of the cognitive system on the perceptual system, of what we "know" on what we "see," and, even as surely, this effect must be due to experience.

NOTE: This research was supported, in part, by the United States Office of Education, Cooperative Research Project No. 3293.

But figural organization does not lend itself easily to study — the problems of stimulus specification and quantification are enormous and comprise a separate study in their own right. Thus the narrower purpose of this paper: to provide a framework in which such changes can be studied.

The problem to be suggested is representative of the class and is amenable to fairly precise study. It is not an obvious problem, however, and requires careful description in the adult before its development can be understood. Most of the remainder of the paper, therefore, will be concerned with this task. It will be shown that knowledge of the structure of language (which must be acquired) affects the perception of words in that language (or letter arrays approximating that language) in adults. Since this is probably the most difficult and controversial aspect of the problem, it has been the focus of the work to be reported.

There is an additional motive to this attempt — to bring the study of perceptual development into conversations concerning modern models of the adult perceptual system. The models which describe perceptual analysis as information processing are of particular relevance. These models, which use such concepts as short-term storage, coding processes, long-term storage (memory), and read-in and read-out processes, have had little or no impact on the literature of perceptual development. But the question of the development of such systems in the adult is clearly relevant and of importance.

A Paradigm for the Study

In their study of the microgenetic growth of the perception of words, Haber and Hershenson (1965) employed an experimental paradigm which has promise for the study of perceptual shifts with cognition. They flashed seven-letter, frequent English words for about 25 msec. per flash in a tachistoscope. For each word, the flashes were repeated, up to 25 times, without changing any of the stimulus parameters. The Ss were instructed to report the letters they were certain they perceived and the positions of those letters.

Phenomenal report of the Ss indicated the following sequence of events: The first flash was usually blank. Parts of letters and whole letters began to appear with the second and third flashes; with more exposures, a number of letters were apparent, and, in some cases, the entire word was seen. The percept of the word that developed with repeated exposures was in no sense fuzzy, hazy, or the product of a guess. It was clear, and S was

111

never uncertain about his report. Counting letters correct or words correct corroborated the phenomenal report — there was a gradual increase with increase in number of exposures.

Haber (1965) improved on this paradigm by forcing a nonsense condition for the guess response. He showed Ss both rare and frequent English words, half of which were exposed for 5 seconds before the first flash. During this time, S was required to spell the word aloud. Haber argued that since S knew the word to be flashed, the probability of selecting it for the response was 1.00. Prior knowledge of the stimulus did make the exposed words easier to perceive, but the difference between rare and frequent words found for the nonexposed words disappeared. The microgenetic effect, the increase in perceptibility with repeated exposures, remained as a perceptual effect.

This paradigm, then, ensures that the responses are "reports" of perceptual experience in Natsoulas's (1967) sense that they represent events occurring in the visual experience of the viewer. This assertion is of such importance * that a brief review of the arguments in support of it is in order. (A more detailed account may be found in Haber, 1966.)

Instructions. Ss are instructed not to guess but to report as carefully as possible what they see. They are required to report letters rather than words. Both instructions increase the probability of getting a perceptual report. If S were instructed to guess, then, surely, perceptual report would be confounded with guesses; instruction not to guess, at the least, decreases the proportion of guesses and brings response closer to report.

Method. Stimuli are presented in a modified method of constant stimuli where the number of exposures per word is predetermined. In this procedure S does not have so much control over the state of his response as in the frequently used method of limits. In the limits procedure S can have as many opportunities to view the stimulus as he needs (or wants) and, when he is uncertain, can simply wait for another exposure — that is, he can suppress his response. Since S cannot predict how many times he will see a particular stimulus in the modified method of constant stimuli, he must report all that he saw after each exposure or risk not having another chance. Moreover, exposing the word before a trial gives S complete knowledge about the stimulus. He has no uncertainty about the word and

---

* Baddeley's (1946) critique of Miller, Bruner, and Postman (1954) illustrates the importance of the distinction between "response" and "report" in the study of the perception of letter arrays.

should not suppress his response. Indeed, the probability of saying the correct word would be 1.00. If something less than 1.00 is obtained, the notion that the responses were perceptually determined would be reinforced.

Response analysis. Analysis of the distributional and sequential properties of the responses can also supply information about their source. The frequency distribution of letters can be compared with known distributions, such as those obtained in visual and auditory confusability studies or tallies of the frequency of letters in English prose.

Likewise, sequential properties of the responses yield evidence for perceptual report. For example, suppose S has reported a letter a few times (say on exposures n, $n + 1$, and $n + 2$). The S knows that the letter is in the stimulus, and, if his report were a reflection of memory, he would report the letter on any and all subsequent exposures. But if the letter is reported on a given exposure and not on the subsequent exposure (which is frequently the case), then one would say that the report is more characteristic of perception than of memory. The same argument holds for the fact that S does not report the whole stimulus on the first flash — that is, immediately after he has seen the stimulus array for 5 seconds and has spelled it aloud. Extending the argument further suggests that even naive Ss, or Ss with poor memories, by some number of exposures, say 10 or 15, should have learned all of the letters in the array and, therefore, should report all of the letters correctly. If the rate of correct responses reaches asymptote at some value under 100 per cent correct, then the responses may be taken to indicate perceptual report.

The Problem

The specific problem to be suggested for developmental study is a consequence of a study of the effect of meaning on the microgenetic growth of perception. Using English and Turkish words as stimuli, Hershenson and Haber (1965) varied cognitive structure in order to assess its effects on perception. The English words were assumed to be related to cognitive structure (memory) already possessed by S. The Turkish words were assumed to have the same or similar internal structure as the English words but with no possibility of being related to cognitive structure available to S. Thus, stimulus structure was controlled to the extent that the languages have unique but equivalent statistical properties.

The procedure used in this study was the same as that of Haber and

113

Hershenson (1965). The words were flashed for some predetermined number of exposures with *S* responding after each flash. The English words were easier to see than the Turkish words, but the microgenetic effect held up for both populations of stimuli. Thus, perceptual growth occurred for meaningful as well as meaningless stimuli and therefore was assumed to be a perceptual effect which was independent of cognitive structure — that is, cognitive structure was not necessary for it to occur.

Experiment I

This study was an attempt to assess the effects of variation in stimulus structure while holding cognitive structure constant — essentially the reverse of the Turkish word study. This approach is desirable because the structural (statistical) properties of the stimuli are more easily manipulable and more precisely specifiable. At the same time, it allows sampling of stimulus structure at a number of points rather than the mere presence or absence that cognitive structure allows. The stimuli were English words and seven-letter arrays in each of zero-, first-, second-, and third-order of approximation to English (AE). By using different approximations to the letter frequencies and sequential dependencies of English, structural differences reflect how closely the stimuli approach the statistical structure of English which, presumably, is "known" to *S* (i.e., represented in some way in *S*'s memory).

Stimuli. Seventy English words were randomly selected from the 504 of Haber and Hershenson (1965). In addition, four lists of 70 seven-letter arrays of each of zero-, first-, second-, and third-order AE were constructed according to a procedure outlined by Shannon (1948). Each stimulus array was lettered in black on a white card and in all respects conformed to the stimulus dimensions of Haber and Hershenson (1965).

Procedure. Ten arrays in each of the stimulus lists were assigned to each of seven exposure numbers (1, 2, 3, 4, 5, 10, and 15) representing the number of times an array would be flashed. Seventy arrays were presented in each of five sessions; two at each of the 35 list-by-exposure-number combinations. The arrays were presented in random order within sessions. The sequence of presenting arrays from the five lists was randomly determined for each *S*. The interval between flashes was never less than five seconds.

The stimuli were presented in one channel of a three-channel mirror tachistoscope (Scientific Prototype Mfg. Corp., Model GA). A second channel, serving as an adapting field, contained two faint lines for fixation boundaries. The S was instructed to fixate between two faint dots, each of which bisected a line. The S initiated each exposure by pressing a button when he was giving maximal attention to the proper fixation point. The reflectance, measured at the eyepiece with a Macbeth Illuminometer, was 95 mL. for both stimulus and adapting fields.

The Ss were trained to report letters rather than words in two practice sessions preceding the experiment. English words with one letter missing were flashed, and S was required to report the letters that he saw on each exposure. Thus, S's performance could be monitored via reports of missing letters. Few incorrect responses were made.

The duration to be used for each S in the experiment proper was determined during these practice sessions by adjusting the exposure duration of the practice arrays until a value was found such that S reported few letters on the first flash but correctly reported all the letters (and the correct missing letter) on some subsequent trial (mean duration $= 12$ msec.).

In all experimental sessions, S reported after each flash both the letters he was certain he perceived and their respective positions even when, in the case of English words, he was certain of the word. At no time was S given information about his accuracy. Nor did he know at the time he was reporting whether the array would be exposed again.

Subjects. The Ss were 11 male undergraduate students enrolled in an elementary course in perception at the University of Wisconsin. They had not previously served in a perception experiment and were not aware of the nature of the experiment at the time of testing. Each S was tested separately in seven 1-hour sessions.

Results. When scored for "words" perceived (all seven letters correct) over the 15 exposures, or letters perceived over the first 5 exposures (Fig. 1), percentage correct was a function of AE, $F(4, 40) = 187.03, p<.01$, with English words the most easily perceived, random letters the least easily perceived, and the other AE's at the appropriate intermediate levels. The microgenetic development of the percept over repeated exposures, $F(4, 40) = 37.57, p<.01$, occurred for each AE in a more or less parallel fashion.

The main effect of position appears to be a combination of a number of factors. In general, the letter in the third position (the one just to the left of fixation) was perceived most often. The letters to the left of fixation were more frequently perceived than those to the right of fixation, and the

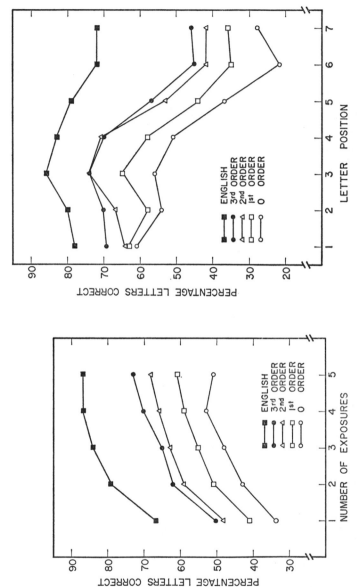

Figure 1. Percentage of letters perceived over the first five exposures as a function of the number of exposures, with order of approximation to English as the parameter, for Experiment I. *Figure 2.* Percentage of letters perceived over the first five exposures as a function of letter position, with order of approximation to English as the parameter, for Experiment I.

end letters (positions 1 and 7) were perceived more frequently than their immediate neighbors. The linear, cubic, and quartic trends for position were all significant.

Letter position interacted with both AE, F (24, 240) $= 16.28$, p$<$.01, and number of exposures, F (24, 240) $= 5.43$, p$<$.01. Figure 2 shows the differential position effect for AE. With respect to position, the curve for English is most nearly symmetrical, whereas the zero-order curve shows a marked left-to-right decrease. The curves for the other AE's fall in between.

In order to analyze the statistical properties of the responses, three frequency distributions were obtained for each exposure-by-approximation cell: (a) letters correctly perceived (e.g., the number of times "A" was given in response to A in the stimulus), (b) stimulus letters confused or incorrectly perceived (e.g., the number of times A was presented but the response was some letter other than "A"), and (c) letters guessed (e.g., the number of times "A" was the response but not the stimulus). The three distributions were essentially summations of portions of a confusion matrix mapping stimuli along the columns into responses along the rows. Letters correct is given by the diagonal entries, letters confused is got by summing the off-diagonal column entries, and letters guessed is got by summing the off-diagonal row entries. The distributions of letters correct and letters confused were converted to percentages, since the letters were not presented an equal number of times. Seventy-five distributions were obtained in this manner.

Partial correlation coefficients were calculated for each of the 75 distributions with 5 other distributions: 3 of visual confusability $-$ 1 objective (VCO) from Chase and Posner (1965) and 2 subjective, (VCS-1) from Tinker (1928) and (VCS-2) from Chase and Posner (1965); 1 of auditory confusability (AC) from Conrad (1964); and English Frequency (EF) from Fitts and Switzer (1962). (Partial correlations were used, since these 5 distributions intercorrelate somewhat.) None of the correlations with AC or with VCS-2 were significant, only 2 of the 75 correlated significantly ($p<$.05) with VCS-1, and only 7 correlated significantly ($p<$.05) with VCO $-$ 5 were letters-correct distributions and 2 were distributions of letters confused.

The correlations with EF are shown in the table on page 118. Of 25 correlations for each distribution, there were 5 significant correlations with letters correct, 16 negative correlations with letters confused, and 20 with letters guessed. The only consistent pattern with letters correct is the higher correlations in the zero-order — that is, for random letters there was a tendency for the more frequent letters in English to be correctly perceived. The pattern for letters confused is confusing: all of the correlations for zero-order and for Exposure 2 are significant, 4 of the 5 for third-order are significant, and 3 of the 5 for Exposure 1 and for English are significant. However, the nonsignificant entries for both letters correct and for letters confused are quite small and do not show consistent trends. The negative correlations for zero-order lend support for the results from letters correct. One might summarize the results for letters confused by saying that when errors were made, there was a tendency to confuse the less frequent letters. It is difficult, however, to explain both of the patterns. Together, they seem to indicate that letters correctly perceived had little relation to the statistical properties of the language and therefore were probably related to visual processes. The seeming contradiction is that the errors were more frequently made on the less frequent

Partial Correlations, by Exposure, between English Frequency and Percentage of Letters Correct, Percentage of Letters Confused, and Frequency of Letters Guessed for Letter Arrays of Varying Order of Approximation to English

Partial Correlations of English Frequency	Order of Approximation to English				
	0	1	2	3	English
With percentage of letters correct					
Exposure 1 ...	.52*	−.04	−.02	−.05	−.18
Exposure 2 ...	.42	−.14	.06	.57**	−.08
Exposure 3 ...	.35	.09	−.07	.48*	−.06
Exposure 4 ...	.42*	.10	.43	.35	−.11
Exposure 5 ...	.62**	−.19	−.28	.29	.07
With percentage of letters confused					
Exposure 1 ...	−.54**	−.79**	−.04	−.62**	−.46
Exposure 2 ...	−.50*	−.49*	−.75**	−.54*	−.56*
Exposure 3 ...	−.61**	−.03	.13	−.48*	−.55*
Exposure 4 ...	−.56**	−.07	−.52*	−.67**	−.29
Exposure 5 ...	−.55**	−.06	−.10	−.23	.67**
With frequency of letters guessed					
Exposure 1 ...	.40	.68**	.71**	.66**	.56*
Exposure 2 ...	.35	.62**	.63**	.59**	.61**
Exposure 3 ...	.33	.66**	.68**	.61**	.51*
Exposure 4 ...	.38	.57**	.60**	.53*	.59*
Exposure 5 ...	.32	.57**	.58**	.51*	.55*

*$p < .05$
**$p < .01$

letters, therefore being directly related to the statistical properties of the stimulus. In light of the strong position effect, one could probably say that for a letter to be perceived, *where* it is is more important than *what* it is.

On the other hand, the pattern for letters guessed is quite clear: Only the zero-order entries were nonsignificant, and these were in the same direction as the others and narrowly missed significance. Thus the distribution of incorrect responses was similar to that of English frequency. The *S*s, when they made errors (were not correct), responded as if they were guessing by sampling from a distribution of English frequency.

That there were no significant correlations between AC and any of the distributions is noteworthy. It suggests that Sperling's (1960; 1963) conception of an auditory rehearsal component of visual perceptual processing may not be applicable to all perceptual tasks.

Experiment II

Except for the 5 seconds during which *S* spelled the stimulus aloud, the letter arrays in Experiment I were relatively unfamiliar to *S*. Thus, it could be argued that, despite the effort to ensure a perceptual set and perceptual responding, the responses reflected characteristics of memory or of response processes. Therefore, a second experiment was performed to minimize such a possibility by requiring *S* to memorize the entire set of letter arrays which would be used in the experiment.

Stimuli. The stimuli were 65 arrays, 13 from each of the five lists of Experiment I. Because of an alteration in the apparatus, the arrays were relettered to be slightly smaller in height, using a LeRoy lettering stencil No. 3240-240C and pen No. 3233-5. All other parameters of stimulation were unchanged.

Procedure. Each *S* was given a set of cards containing the 65 arrays to memorize at his leisure. When *S* felt he had committed the list to memory, he was tested in the tachistoscope to determine whether he could reproduce the arrays, given only a brief look at them (approximately 10 msec.). When *S* was able to reproduce from memory over 95 per cent of the letters in all of the arrays, he was permitted to begin the experiment proper. During the test sessions, *E* was able to determine the duration at which *S* saw few letters on a single flash, the duration used thereafter in the experiment proper (mean duration $= 20$ msec.).

The 65 arrays were each exposed five times according to ten independently constructed, random orders. These orders were sequenced randomly over ten days so that all Ss tested on the same day (never more than three) received the same list on that day. However, since Ss started the experiment on different days, no two Ss received the same sequence of random lists — the random order of lists and experimental day on which a particular S would receive the lists were uncorrelated.

The Ss were given prior knowledge of the stimulus array to be flashed by exposing the array in the tachistoscope and requiring S to call out the letters. This procedure, together with complete learning of the stimulus population, should eliminate any differential forgetting for arrays of different AE. In all other ways the procedure was the same as in Experiment I.

Subjects. The seven Ss were the author and six graduate and undergraduate students who were paid for participating in the experiment. Three Ss were familiar with the procedure, the remainder were not.

Results. Although letters correct increased as a function of number of exposures (F (4, 24) $= 5.04$, $p < .01$), the major portion of the effect occurred over the first three exposures (Fig. 3). The microgenetic development of the percept again occurred in a parallel fashion for each AE, F (4, 24) $= 9.81$, $p < .01$. The overall level of the effect was, once again, ordered within each exposure according to AE, with English yielding the highest values, and zero-order the lowest, but the ordering was not

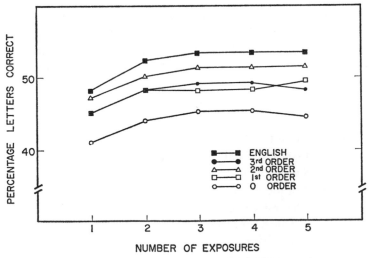

Figure 3. Percentage of letters perceived as a function of the number of exposures, with order of approximation to English as the parameter, for Experiment II.

quite the same as in Experiment I: third-order now dropped to a position equivalent to that of first-order.

Letter position was again significant, F (6, 60) $= 23.75$, $p<.01$, but presents a markedly different picture from that of Experiment I. Although the interactions of Position with AE and Exposures were significant, both curves overlapped a great deal — that is, all the curves showed more or less the same overall function. Figure 4 shows the comparative main effects of Position; the curve for Experiment I masks a great deal of spread among the various AE's (see Fig. 2), but that for Experiment II is highly representative. The difference between the two experiments for the Position by AE interaction is that in Experiment II the linear and cubic trends were not significant whereas the quadratic trend was significant, F_q (1, 6) $= 43.47$, $p<.01$. This means that even though there were differences among the AE's, the shape of the function in all cases was more like what one would expect from a perceptual system: highest perceptibility at fixation, dropping off the farther a letter was from the fixation point.

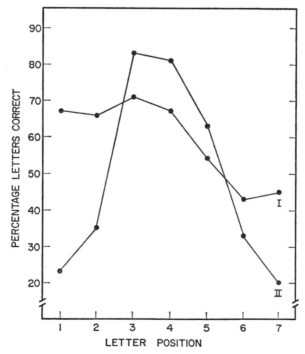

Figure 4. Percentage of letters perceived as a function of letter position for Experiments I and II.

121

The interaction with number of exposures did show some consistency in this case. For the first few exposures, improvement in perception was greatest for the positions to the right of fixation, and for the last few it was greatest to the left. No clear pattern could be discerned for the interaction of exposures with AE.

An analysis of errors was impossible to perform, since Ss made almost no errors at all — they reported either correct letters or nothing. The distribution for letters correct was available for analysis, but no consistent patterns were discernible. For the 125 distributions, only three r's were significant.

Experiment III

In general, then, Experiment II suggests that the more closely a stimulus approximates the structure in memory, the better it is perceived. Experiment III is aimed at discovering the processes underlying this phenomenon. Recent conceptions of the temporal course of perceptual processing (e.g., Sperling, 1963; Averbach & Sperling, 1961) provide a reasonable context for this analysis. Stimulus information is stored intact for a short period of time in a fast-decaying memory (short-term visual storage). During this interval, the information is "read-out" of this store and coded for efficient storage in a longer lasting memory. It would probably be reasonable to suppose that the effect of cognition on perception takes place during the coding phase rather than the early, complete-storage phase, if coding occurs before experience.

These processes can be studied by sampling stimulus information available to S at various times after stimulus onset. Since perception is an event taking place over time, an indicator can be flashed some time after stimulus onset, and S can be asked to report the letter in the indicated position. The transformations on the input that occur over time yield information about process. Unfortunately, this experiment has to be run in three parts, the first of which is complete enough to see the trend.

Procedure. The stimuli were 70 letter arrays varying in AE, the same ones used in Experiment II. An indicator marker — a small vertical black line presented in a second channel of the tachistoscope which appeared to S to be ⅛ inch above the indicated letter — informed S which letter to report. Because the interstimulus interval (ISI) — that is, the time between the offset of the letter array and the onset of the marker — could not be varied to include all of the necessary conditions, the experiment was divided into three parts. In the first part the indicator was presented in one of two conditions: either simultaneously with the letter array (i.e., both stimulus field and indicator field flashed at the same time) or successively (i.e., the indicator field flashed immediately upon termination of the stimulus field).* The second and third parts will give similar tests at ISI's of 0, 25, 50, 75, and 100 msec. and of 100, 200, 300, 400, and 500 msec.

The duration of the letter arrays and of the indicator were both fixed at 50 msec. The stimulus arrays were randomly sampled for position, for each S. There were three groups of Ss: Naive-Guess, Naive-No Guess, and Trained. The Naive groups knew nothing about the letter arrays before they were flashed. The Trained group memorized the list of stimuli to be shown and, in addition, saw and were required to spell to E the word that would be flashed. No-Guess and Trained Ss were instructed, as in the previous experiments, that they were to report only those letters they were certain they had seen. Guess Ss were forced to make a response even when they did not see a letter. This condition was included to permit comparison with results from other experiments using the indicator methodology. There were 20 Ss in the Naive–No Guess group; 10 were run with and 10 without a partial mask over the stimuli to test for masking. There were 10 Ss in the Naive-Guess group. The Trained group data were constructed from 2 Trained Ss who were run on 5 replications each.

Results. As expected from the model, no differences were found for letters correctly perceived among the four AE's and English, $F (4, 60) = 1.86$, $p < .05$, nor was there any difference between the simultaneous and successive conditions, $F (1, 15) < 1.00$. Whatever effect structured memory has on perception, therefore, appears to take place some time after the stimulus is turned off.

Summary and Conclusions

My purpose has been to demonstrate that a problem exists which has received little attention from developmental psychologists although it is clearly of great importance. The effect of acquired cognitive structure on perception has been clearly demonstrated, and a method for studying the processes underlying the effect has been described. It would be intriguing

* Contrast reduction owing to luminance summation was clearly visible in the simultaneous condition but did not alter performance: no difference was found between scores obtained when there was no overlap between the two stimulus fields and scores obtained with complete overlap. There was no evidence of masking in the successive condition.

to speculate about the development of a system which codes information for storage over long periods of time. Even more fascinating are the developmental alternatives for the effects of the stored material on the incoming information — for this is the nature of the effect with which I have been concerned. But speculation without data is of little value. The direction for study of this and similar phenomena seems to be clear: the mechanisms mediating the effects of cognition on perception must be worked out both for the adult and for the child. To be sure, the study of the child will provide problems of greater difficulty than those already encountered with adults. Perceptual "reports" of children are more difficult to interpret; classes of stimuli that are appropriate for children are more difficult to ascertain. But this is invariably true, and the difficulties will be overcome.

References

Averbach, E., & G. Sperling. Short-term storage of information in vision; in C. Cherry, ed., *Symposium on information theory*, pp. 196–211. London: Butterworth, 1961.

Baddeley, A. D. Immediate memory and the "perception" of letter sequences. *Quarterly Journal of Experimental Psychology*, 1964, 16, 364–367.

Chase, W., & M. I. Posner. The effect of auditory and visual confusability on visual and memory search tasks. Paper read at Midwestern Psychological Association, Chicago, May 1965.

Conrad, R. Acoustic confusions in immediate memory. *British Journal of Psychology*, 1964, 55, 75–84.

Fitts, P. M., & G. Switzer. Cognitive aspects of information processing: I. The familiarity of S-R sets and subsets. *Journal of Experimental Psychology*, 1962, 63, 321–329.

Haber, R. N. The effect of prior knowledge of the stimulus on word recognition processes. *Journal of Experimental Psychology*, 1965, 69, 282–286.

————. Perceptual recognition: The direct effect of repetition, duration, frequency, and prior knowledge. Paper read at Psychonomic Society, St. Louis, October 1966.

————, & M. Hershenson. Effects of repeated brief exposures on the growth of a percept. *Journal of Experimental Psychology*, 1965, 69, 40–46.

Hershenson, M., & R. N. Haber. The role of meaning in the perception of briefly exposed words. *Canadian Journal of Psychology*, 1965, 19, 42–46.

Miller, G. A., J. S. Bruner, & L. Postman. Familiarity of letter sequences and tachistoscopic identification. *Journal of General Psychology*, 1954, 50, 129–139.

Natsoulas, T. What are perceptual reports about? *Psychological Bulletin*, 1967, 67, 249–272.

Shannon, C. L. A mathematical theory of communication. *Bell System Technical Journal*, 1948, 27, 379–423, 623–656.

Sperling, G. The information available in brief visual presentations. *Psychological Monographs*, 1960, 74, No. 11 (Whole No. 498).

————. A model for visual memory tasks. *Human Factors*, 1963, 5, 19–31.

Tinker, M. A. The relative legibility of the letters, the digits, and of certain mathematical signs. *Journal of General Psychology*, 1928, 1, 472–493.

◈ WAYNE H. HOLTZMAN, ROGELIO DIAZ-GUERRERO ◈
JON D. SWARTZ, AND LUIS LARA TAPIA

Cross-Cultural Longitudinal Research on Child Development: Studies of American and Mexican Schoolchildren

ONE of the most significant developments in contemporary psychology is the rapid growth of cross-cultural research on a scale unheard of a decade ago. The widening search for cultural variation, the growing realization of parochial limitations of psychology in the United States, the increased communication among behavioral scientists from many disciplines and nations, the development of technology and resources making large-scale research feasible — all contribute greatly to this new kind of comparative psychology, a comparative psychology of human behavior in markedly different natural settings rather than of different animal species.

NOTE: The research reported herein was made possible by research grant M-3223 from the United States Public Health Service and by research grant 63-282 from the Foundations Fund for Research in Psychiatry. The authors wish to thank the following people who participated in the research program as examiners and assistants: Charles Brasfield, Shirley Cone, Bobby Farrow, Gail Gordon, Ruth Isely, Connie Kitley, Don Laird, Luis Laosa, Thomas Mandeville, Rodney McGinnis, Jane Stitt, Carol Swartz, and Donald Witzke at the University of Texas, and René Ahumada, Guiliana de Astis Arlotta, Gustavo Fernández P., Maria de la Luz Fernández D., Brenda Marcela Ré, Maria Luisa Morales Castillo, Isabel Reyes de Ahumada, Angel San Román, Piedad Aladro Lubel, Elda Alicia Alba Canto, Elena Sommer L., Martha Eugenia Peña Ledesma, Eric Lizt, Dyrna Gladys García, and Isabel Jaidar Matalobos of the National University of Mexico. Special thanks are due Joseph S. Thorpe of Emory University for major assistance in the early stages of this project when he was closely associated with it as a faculty member at the University of Texas.

125

Cross-cultural, comparative approaches are particularly appealing for the study of sociocultural factors in any aspect of human development. Different patterns of child rearing, variations in family life-style, contrasting value systems, sociolinguistic variations, as well as different social orders and their political or economic systems are but a few of the major environmental influences upon human development that require a cross-cultural approach if one is to study them under real life conditions. In spite of the obvious appeal of cross-cultural approaches to human development, conceptual and methodological difficulties encountered in such research have, until recently, been so forbidding that psychologists have generally left the field of sociocultural comparison to anthropologists and social theorists.

The beginning field research in culture and personality is generally attributed to Margaret Mead's monumental study, *Coming of Age in Samoa* (1928), and the provocative work of Bronislaw Malinowski, *Sex and Repression in Savage Society* (1927). These early studies of child development and family patterns created a sensation throughout the world because of their dramatic implications for psychoanalytic theory. In the ensuing years, numerous anthropologists undertook similar psychodynamic case studies of personality development in exotic cultures. Many of these investigators employed the Rorschach or a variation of the Thematic Apperception Test to probe the depths of the aborigine psyche in the manner of a clinician, hoping thereby to gain insight into the modal personality of a given culture. Kaplan (1961) estimated that over a hundred and fifty studies in 75 societies had employed projective techniques in the period 1940–1960 alone. The net outcome of these cross-cultural personality studies employing projective techniques has been disappointing because of major flaws present in most of the studies and the techniques (Lindzey, 1961).

One can hardly criticize the anthropologist for failing to solve what are essentially conceptual and methodological problems of a psychological nature. If the psychologist wishes to investigate certain sociocultural factors in personality development, he must develop cross-cultural settings for his own research and must deal directly with the issues rather than sidestepping them. Considering the present state of development characteristic of most psychological techniques for personality assessment, it is probably premature to expect much to be gained from their application in nonliterate societies.

WAYNE H. HOLTZMAN

Some Major Issues in Cross-Cultural Psychological Studies of Child Development

Most cross-cultural studies by psychologists consist of a simple, approximate replication in one culture of a study originally conducted in another. Such replication follows naturally from a desire to see how well a given approach works in another country or language. Usually, enough significant variation in method is inadvertently introduced to reduce markedly the value of the second study as a controlled replication. Although such cross-cultural extensions are desirable in their own right, little can be said about the cultural factors per se as they may or may not influence human development. In such casual replications, little attention is given to problems of sampling, linguistic equivalence of meaning, examiner variability, and cultural variation in response set. Moreover, a theoretical rationale for undertaking the cross-cultural study in the first place is notably absent in most cases. The deliberate introduction of a cultural variable as part of the original research design is quite another matter, calling for considerable care and ingenuity to deal with the greatly increased complexity of the problem.

Quite aside from the general problems confronting an investigator of child development, certain issues are peculiar to cross-cultural research (Holtzman, 1965). The kinds of cultural variables that are present; the generalization desired; the problem of maintaining semantic equivalence of techniques across cultures, including examiner variability and cultural variation in response set as well as translation of the language; and the theoretical issue of how much the manifestations of personality are inextricably bound up in language constitute four issues of special concern which will be discussed individually.

CULTURAL VARIABLES

To have meaning as a cross-cultural study, a plan for research must deal first with the fundamental questions, What cultural variables are present? and Why are they important? The Whitings (1960) have outlined three aspects of the concept of culture: First is the body of knowledge transmitted from one generation to the next about how to do things or how to get things done — the techniques of the society. Second is the belief system of the culture, the ethnoscientific and religious dogma. And third is the ethical system or set of values that provides guidance about what is good or bad, what is important or trivial, and the relative merits of various goals and behaviors in a hierarchical sense. Together, the techniques, beliefs, and values form the custom complex, a blueprint for action or cognitive map of organized roles in institutional settings. Of special interest is the life-style of the individual as he relates to his family, his peer group, or other aspects of his society. By this definition, a given nation, such as the United States or Mexico, may have wide variations in culture within its own borders, even granting a common language or dominant culture which sets the tone for the nation as a whole.

An example of a cultural variable is the degree of dependency of the child upon the mother, which is characteristically valued and fostered by child-rearing patterns within the society. In some cultures, a high degree of dependency is encouraged, whereas in others, the child's early independence of the mother is enforced. Since mother-child interaction is present in all societies, degree of dependency is a universal cultural variable that, conceivably, can be measured in any society. In studying this variable as it may influence personality development, one can imagine a research design calling for random sampling of cases from hundreds of societies representing wide variation in degree of dependency. Such a pancultural design is unfeasible in practice, although approximations to it have been made by Whiting and Child (1953) from descriptive data on many cultures recorded in the Human Relations Area Files. The primary difficulty with such an approach is that the available data are woefully inadequate, having been collected for other purposes. Moreover, the use of correlation coefficients between the variable of special interest and anything else that may be universally available often results in superficial statistical relations that are impossible to interpret.

If one narrows his interest to literate societies for which some psychological measures may already have been accumulated, the range of variation in the cultural variables is necessarily restricted. For some cultural variables, the restriction to literate societies completely eliminates the cross-cultural variation. Nevertheless, sufficient variation still exists on many important cultural dimensions when only literate societies are employed to make significant contributions to the psychological study of human development. But a few of the numerous cultural variables * pres-

---

* A distinction should be made here between cross-national and cross-cultural research. Considerable cultural variation usually exists within a single nation, particularly in larger countries with major regional differences. Sometimes the term *subculture* is employed to denote relatively minor cultural variation within one country. For this reason, it is usually rather misleading to speak of "national char-

ent in modern societies are patterns of child rearing, modal family life-style, acceptable ways of channeling aggression, internalized mechanisms of behavioral control, degree of competitive striving, importance of kinship and other affiliative patterns, and the degree of active coping with stress to gain mastery of the environment.

Determining what cultural variables are present in societies tentatively chosen for study involves much more than merely observing variation on a particular dimension of interest. Just as two individuals will differ on an almost infinite number of variables, so will two societies differ in many characteristics besides the one in question. Careful cross-cultural matching on relevant subcultural dimensions, such as father's occupation or amount of education, will reduce considerably the number of uncontrolled cultural variables, but in the last analysis, there will still be some which must be carefully weighed in any interpretation of empirical results. The investigator must make such variables as explicit as possible, even though they cannot be rigorously controlled.

CROSS-CULTURAL GENERALIZATION

Ideally, one would like to draw conclusions about the general influence of a major cultural variable upon human development — conclusions applicable to mankind as a whole. Only a pancultural design, drawing a large, representative sample from the universe of cultures, will permit such broad generalizations. Unavailability of pertinent, valid psychological data on a wide range of cultures precludes the use of pancultural designs except in studies severely limited in scope. The task of designing and executing a truly pancultural design where fresh data are systematically collected under standard conditions is so forbidding that no one has attempted it.

More realistic than the pancultural approach is one in which a limited sample of cultures is drawn — those that maximize desired variation in a dimension of special interest. Whiting and his colleagues (1963) chose six different cultures, ranging from a village in New England to an African tribe in Kenya, and conducted field studies on child-rearing practices and

acter" or to oversimplify by gross comparisons of "Americans" and "Mexicans." For many cultural factors, the variation within either Mexico or the United States is much greater than the variation between the two countries. One must keep in mind, however, that true cross-national differences may exist in some isolated variables and in the functional patterning of other variables which, examined one at a time, show no differences.

personality development. Although similar methods were used in each study, the outcome has been rather disappointing from a psychological point of view. Working only with literate cultures, the Andersons (1962) studied children's moral values in nine different countries, using an incomplete story method to elicit fantasy material. A basic problem with most such investigations is that significant international differences may be due to any number of inadvertently ignored cultural variables other than the one or two dimensions in which the investigator professes interest.

Most common of all is the cross-cultural study of only two cultures. Here the possibilities for misinterpretation are even greater. The situation is not unlike a clinician's comparing two individuals in the hope of gaining insight into a psychodynamic mechanism — an intensive case study of each person (or the repeated measurement of key variables in each person under various conditions) provides rich insight into the individual as a functioning organism but hardly permits any generalization to others without replication. Although universal hypotheses about culture and personality cannot be tested in a bicultural design, limited hypotheses about subcultural variation and social factors within culture can be examined effectively.

The systematic use of subcultural variation, replicated across two or more cultures, is the most promising approach for the psychological study of cultural factors in child development. Extensive within-nation heterogeneity can be included by deliberately sampling a range of socioeconomic, ethnic, and life-style variables. Within most nations, enough sociocultural variation occurs to permit cross-national matching of many important subcultural variables, so it is much easier to interpret the outcome of any major cross-cultural findings. Such methods are well known and commonly accepted when applied within a single country; applying them to two or more countries at a time is far more difficult, though clearly feasible in many instances. The study by Rosen (1964) of achievement motivation and the sociocultural factors that influence it in Brazil and the United States is a good example of a bicultural design that takes full advantage of subcultural variation. His generalizations are, of course, limited to these two cultures.

The issues involved in selection of an appropriate generalization to be drawn from a cross-cultural design are only partially resolved by cross-cultural matching on subcultural variation. In the last analysis, one must always exercise considerable caution in attributing significant differences to presumed cultural factors.

SEMANTIC EQUIVALENCE OF MEASUREMENT TECHNIQUES

A major problem too often ignored is the different meaning a given psychological test or interview question may have in two different cultures. Where two or more different languages are spoken, the need for translation is obvious. But for some techniques employed in the study of child development, even a skillful translation is not enough. On such subtests of the Wechsler Intelligence Scale for Children as Information, Vocabulary, or Comprehension, for example, individual items will be inappropriate unless completely rewritten. Even many nonverbal tests will have questionable validity in another culture unless they are altered specifically for that culture.

Since a measurement technique can never be divorced from the context in which it is administered, a number of other considerations arise besides the adequacy of translation. Variation in examiner style is a case in point. A mental set to respond in a particular fashion must also be taken into account. A child in one culture may be familiar with psychological tests or with adults' asking certain questions, whereas a child in another culture may view such techniques with suspicion and see them as strange or threatening. The syntax of the investigator's relationship with the child must be examined carefully. Unlike the ethnographer, who is a member of a society different from his informants', the psychological examiner or interviewer should be a member of the society in which he is working. In cross-cultural studies, this consideration means that close collaboration between psychologists in each of the cultures is essential.

THE SAME PERSONALITY IN DIFFERENT LANGUAGES

An important theoretical issue is the extent to which manifestations of personality are tied inextricably to language. The Whorfian hypothesis is that differences in linguistic habit cause differences in nonlinguistic behavior. Although evidence bearing upon this provocative hypothesis is still highly ambiguous (Rubenstein & Aborn, 1960), a recent study by Ervin (1964) suggests that some aspects of personality do indeed look different when one language is used for responding to a psychological test than when another is used by the same person. Ervin gave selected cards of the Thematic Apperception Test to sixty-four bilingual Frenchmen on two different occasions, once in English and once in French. The response content and associated personality variables shifted significantly from one language to the other in ways that were predictable from knowledge of the two cultures.

To the extent that this phenomenon generally occurs across languages, important manifestations of personality may be difficult to interpret, regardless of other precautions taken. Until further work is done on this problem with additional samples of bilingual subjects, we have to qualify cross-cultural interpretations of personality by admitting that at least some of the obtained differences could be the result of linguistic differences of expression as well as semantic variations, cultural variability in the meaning of examiner-subject interactions, or cultural differences in response set.

These four theoretical and methodological issues do not exhaust the problems encountered by a psychologist conducting cross-cultural studies of child development. In addition to the special issues peculiar to cross-cultural designs, there are the usual difficulties in measuring relevant aspects of personality, motivation, perception, and cognitive behavior.

Where one is concerned with developmental processes through time, repeated testing in a longitudinal design is essential. Problems in longitudinal studies, such as practice and selective attrition, are well known to most investigators and need not be explored further here. The advantages of a longitudinal, developmental approach to the study of intelligence, cognitive style, and personality have been discussed elsewhere (Holtzman, 1966).

When the sheer difficulties of mounting a major cross-cultural longitudinal study of child development are added to the major issues described above, one might well ask whether such research is really worth the effort. Granted that generalizations must be limited and tentative, pending further replications, and that rigorous cross-cultural designs can only be approximately implemented at best, the situation is not quite so discouraging as it may at first appear. Even in a bicultural study, a great deal of insight can be gained into the role of specified cultural variables in human development, provided that care is taken to include subcultural variations which can be matched cross-culturally, to employ well-trained native examiners who have been calibrated cross-culturally, to use only techniques that can be reasonably defended in both cultures, and, most important of all, to secure the close and continual collaboration of seasoned, native investigators who are fully sensitive to the above issues in both cultures. The remainder of this paper describes such a research program and some of its preliminary findings for schoolchildren in Austin, Texas, and Mexico City.

Description of the Austin–Mexico City Project

The proximity of Texas and Mexico has naturally resulted in considerable professional and scientific interaction among psychologists and other behavioral scientists, particularly between the University of Texas and the National University of Mexico. The large proportion of Spanish-speaking people of Mexican descent in Texas and the heavy influx to Mexico City of North American ideas, products, tourists, scholars, and businessmen have sensitized both groups to the desirability of conducting cross-cultural research before further cultural diffusion and social changes occur.

Periodic exchanges, seminars, and workshops participated in by Mexican and North American psychologists have been taking place since the Third Inter-American Congress of Psychology was held in Austin in 1955. Four Mexican psychologists, led by Rogelio Diaz-Guerrero, spent four months at the University of Texas in 1959 working closely with several American psychologists on the problems of conducting cross-cultural research on personality in the two countries. Considerable time was devoted to problems of translation, standardization, sampling, examiner variability, and the nature of cultural variables present. During the next five years, over one hundred different Mexican students of psychology participated in month-long workshops in Austin, where they had a firsthand look at psychology as taught in the United States, particularly techniques of test construction, personality measurement, and research design. A somewhat smaller group of American psychology students and research assistants from Austin attended similar programs in Mexico City, where they concentrated on learning about variations in Mexican culture and ways to conceptualize some relations between culture and personality. This unusual degree of long-term collaboration and commitment to cross-cultural studies on the part of both Mexicans and Americans has provided a firm basis for the Austin–Mexico City project.

A major part of the impetus for a longitudinal study of cognitive, perceptual, and personality development in children came from successful completion of the basic standardization program for the Holtzman Inkblot Technique (Holtzman, Thorpe, Swartz, & Herron, 1961). Within normal populations ranging from five-year-olds to superior adults, highly significant age trends were found for all but two of the twenty-two individual scores analyzed, as well as for most of the pattern scores derived from genetic level indices in the Rorschach (Thorpe & Swartz, 1965). These cross-sectional results indicated a shift from the impulsive production of diffuse, undifferentiated responses uncritical of form to increasingly mature, well-organized perceptual and ideational activity. Other findings also substantiated in a general way similar studies with the Rorschach. Such cross-sectional comparisons, however, are subject to sampling biases and lack information about changes in individuals over time. The developmental correlates of inkblot scores as well as other perceptual, cognitive, and personality variables can be determined in any rigorous sense only by longitudinal studies using relevant subcultural, family, peer group, and other environmental measures.

RESEARCH DESIGN AND SUBJECTS

An overlapping longitudinal design was employed so that a span of twelve years could be covered in only six calendar years of repeated testing. The basic design is presented in Table 1. The three years of overlap for each of the three groups of children make it possible to correct developmental trends for practice effects, yielding one continuous curve over the ages six to seventeen for each variable studied in each culture. Initial ages for testing were set at 6 years, 8 months, for the youngest group; at 9 years, 8 months, for the middle group; and at 12 years, 8 months, for the oldest group of children. These particular ages were selected so that all testing could be done during the school year. Allowing for some attrition through the six years of repeated testing, it was expected that complete developmental data could be obtained for over six hundred children, three hundred in Austin and a comparable number in Mexico City. Thus,

Table 1. Overlapping Longitudinal Design for Six Years of Repeated
Testing in Austin and Mexico City

Group	Initial Age	No. of Cases		School Grades Covered
		Austin	Mexico	
I	6.7	133	151	1 2 3 4 5 6
II	9.7	142	140	4 5 6 7 8 9
III	12.7	142	152	7 8 9 10 11 12
Total		417	443	

the final Ns of the three age groups would be sufficiently large to permit the application of multivariate analysis for the identification of specific as well as general principles of developmental change.

In Austin, children were drawn mainly from six elementary schools and one junior high school, representing a broad range of working-class, business, and professional families. Children of military personnel, university students, and legislators were eliminated from consideration because of the high likelihood that they would move away before the end of the six-year period. The nature of the study was explained to the parents to secure their permission and cooperation for the repeated testing and interviewing. Only white, English-speaking families were used. The Austin sample probably can be best characterized as consisting of middle-class urban children from fairly stable families who represent the dominant values in American culture.

Defining the sample and selecting children in Mexico City proved to be more difficult, largely because little previous study had been made of the social characteristics of Mexican families and because the organization of education in Mexico is very different from that in the United States. Preliminary pilot studies and demographic surveys had to be undertaken in Mexico City before a detailed sampling plan could be formulated. In addition, the Mexicans had to organize a research group, obtain substantial financial support for a long-range operation, train psychological examiners, and translate test materials before they could embark on the main longitudinal study. For these reasons, there is a three-year lag in the collection of test data; the Austin project was in the middle of its third year of repeated testing when the first year of testing was begun in Mexico.

The preliminary sociological study in Mexico City was undertaken mainly in three school systems, two public and one private. El "Centro," near the center of the city, is one of the oldest public school systems in Mexico City. The area is similar in some ways to the East Side of Manhattan; many current leaders in sports, entertainment, and public life have come out of its *vecindades* and *viviendas*. Although most of the families in El Centro are from the lower class, they are fairly stable. The Independencia school system is located on the edge of the city in one of the fairly new public housing projects designed mainly for working-class people. The private school system in Mexico, usually run by the Catholic elite or clergy, caters mainly to middle-class families where the father is in business or one of the professions. The private schools in this study are typical of the many private systems in Mexico City, and they are most like middle-class urban schools in the United States.

Considerable information about family structure, parental occupation and education, size and quality of the house, and possession of radio or television sets, automobiles, and refrigerators was obtained from interviews with the parents in the preliminary sociological survey. Only children whose parents were both born in Mexico of Mexican parents were included in the sample for the cross-cultural study, to ensure that the dominant Mexican value system and urban life-style would be clearly present. The results of this survey indicated that the Mexican families in the private school system were very similar in socioeconomic status to the American families in Austin. Consequently, twice as many children were drawn from the private school as from El Centro, and about one third of the sample was drawn from Independencia. It was estimated that nearly two thirds of the Mexican and Austin children could be used for cross-cultural comparisons in which important subcultural variations would be matched across the two samples — the remaining one third of the Mexicans would be too low socioeconomically, and the remaining third of the Americans would be too high.

TESTS AND RELATED MEASURES

In addition to the Holtzman Inkblot Technique, the basic test battery includes selected cognitive, perceptual, and personality tests given individually to each child once a year on the anniversary of the initial testing. Criteria employed in deciding whether or not to use a particular test were: (a) suitability for individual administration under field conditions in a school, (b) demonstrated reliability and objectivity from previous studies, (c) appropriateness for use throughout the age span of six to seventeen years, (d) relevance to perceptual-cognitive development or importance as a measure of significant personality traits pertinent to developmental stages in children, and (e) feasibility for use in Spanish and English languages within Mexican and American cultures, respectively.

It was realized that some important psychological techniques might be suitable for administration once or twice; others would be appropriate for use with young children but inappropriate for older ones, or vice versa; and still others worthy of inclusion might come to our attention after a year or two of testing had been completed. Rather than adhere rigidly to a fixed set of measures to be applied uniformly for all six years and in both samples, provision was made for distinguishing among the basic core battery, which is applied uniformly; the partial core battery, which is applied uniformly for all children in the second grade or above; the supplementary repeated battery, consisting of tests employed two or more successive years, though not uniformly; and other measures which are used once or twice but not successively across years. A list of the test batteries and related measures employed in each of these four categories is presented below.

Both forms of the Holtzman Inkblot Technique (HIT) were used to ensure a balanced design, alternating the two parallel forms in successive years. The Human Figure Drawing (HFD) was included because of the earlier work by Witkin et al. (1962), its ease of administration and scoring, and its extensive use in previous cross-cultural studies. Inspection of factor-analytic studies of standard intelligence scales suggested Vocabulary and Block Design in the Wechsler Intelligence Scale for Children (WISC) as the most appropriate subtests to be used repeatedly. For the last two years in Group III, the same subtests from the Wechsler Adult Intelligence Scale are being substituted for the WISC. All testing in Austin will be completed by May 1968, whereas the Mexican data will not be complete until two years later.

In addition to the tests which constituted the basic core battery, a num-

PSYCHOLOGICAL TEST BATTERIES AND RELATED MEASURES

Core Test Battery (all Ss for 6 years)
  Holtzman Inkblot Technique (22 scores)
  Human Figure Drawing (Goodenough score)
  Vocabulary (WISC or WAIS)
  Block Design (WISC or WAIS)
Partial Core Battery (repeatedly for all Ss age 7.7 or older)
  Test Anxiety Scale for Children (1 or 3 scores)
  Time Estimation (3 scores)
  Test Behavior Ratings (5 scores)
Supplementary Repeated Battery (2 or more years)
  Object Sorting Test (first 3 years, 7 scores)
  Embedded Figures Test (all Ss age 9.7 or older, 4 scores)
  Stroop Color-Word Test (Texan Ss age 9.7 or older for 4 years, 2 scores)

Visual Fractionation Test (all Ss for 2 years, 6 scores)
Conceptual Styles Test (ages 7.7 & 8.7 only, 6 scores)
Perceptual Maturity Test (last 3 years, 1 score)
Word Association Test (last 3 years, 7 scores)
Other Measures
  WISC Arithmetic and Picture Completion (all Ss first & fifth years)
  WISC Remaining Subtests (Texans age 6.7 & all Mexicans)
  Family and Home Ratings from Interviews with Mothers
  Parental Attitude Scales (mother)
  Peer Group Sociometric Ratings (first year, Groups I & II)
  Teacher Behavior Rating (fourth year)
  Academic Summary (school record data)

137

ber of other instruments were employed in the first year. All of the first-grade children in Austin were given the complete WISC, whereas the fourth- and seventh-graders were given the Arithmetic and Picture Completion subtests. All the Mexican children were given the complete WISC because little is known about the factorial structure of intelligence in Mexican children. Minor adaptations of the Spanish WISC were necessary to produce semantic equivalence between the English and Spanish versions.* Time Estimation is a short test in which the child is simply requested to estimate the duration of one minute. This test was given on three different occasions during the testing sessions, but was discontinued for first-graders after it was discovered early in the testing that many of them did not know what a minute was.

The Object Sorting Test (OST), a twelve-item form of the Embedded Figures Test (EFT), and the Stroop Color-Word Test (CWT) were also included in the first year, partly because of the earlier work by Gardner (1959) suggesting that they provide important measures of "equivalence range," "field-articulation," and "constricted-flexible control." Moreover, development studies by Witkin et al. (1962) show curvilinear trends for the EFT across ages ten to seventeen, as well as interesting correlates with Rorschach scores. The OST was scored not only for number of categories, as advocated by Gardner, but also according to the Open-Closed and Public-Private dimensions developed by McGaughran and Moran (1956). The latter method yielded scores with significant inkblot correlates in an earlier study of schizophrenic thought processes (Holtzman, Gorham, & Moran, 1964). The Stroop Color-Word Test was not given in Mexico, since doing so would have required new standardization in another language.

Three new tests were employed in the second year: the Conceptual Style Test (CST) and the Visual Fractionation Test (VFT) developed by Kagan and his associates (1963) and the Test Anxiety Scale for Children (TASC; Sarason et al., 1960). The CST was given only to the youngest group of children, but the VFT was given to all three age-groups. In addition, a brief set of rating scales was constructed for use by the examiner in judging the child's test behavior on social confidence, self-confidence in ability, cooperation, general anxiety level, and attention to tasks.

In the third, fourth, and fifth years for the Austin sample, several addi-

* A good discussion of the changes made to adapt the WISC for use in Mexico has been presented by Ahumada, Ahumada, and Diaz-Guerrero (1967).

tional techniques were employed. Most notable of these was the development and application of an extensive interview schedule and parental attitude questionnaire. Interviews lasting one to two hours were conducted with the mother of each child in the sample to determine important characteristics of the home environment and family life-style. Special attention was given to intellectual stimulation and press for achievement given the child by the family, in order to replicate and extend the work of Wolf (1965) on home environment, intelligence, and school achievement. The sixty-eight–item attitude questionnaire was adapted from the work of Hereford (1963) and is similar to other parental attitude scales. A few items of special relevance to cross-cultural attitudes were also included. Two new tests added in the third year and repeated thereafter are Moran's Word Association Test (1966) for which there is now a Spanish version (Moran & Núñez, 1967), and Van de Castle's Perceptual Maturity Test (1965), a seventy-two–item test constructed by pairing selected figures indicative of high and low perceptual maturity from Welsh's Figure Preference Test. Peer group sociometric ratings in the first year, teachers' ratings in the fourth year, and miscellaneous test and behavioral data in the school records complete the available information about the Austin sample through the fifth year of repeated testing.

Cross-Cultural Results for the First Two Years

Most developmental comparisons between the two cultures must await completion of the sixth year of data collection before they can be undertaken as originally planned. In the meantime, some cross-sectional studies for one or two years at a time can be carried out. A cross-cultural comparison of the first year's test results formed the basis for a symposium at the Tenth Inter-American Congress of Psychology in Lima, Peru, in 1966. A summary of some of the more interesting findings is given in the proceedings of the Congress (Diaz-Guerrero, 1967; Lara Tapia, 1967; Swartz, 1967).

Analysis of data for the first two years makes it possible to combine some features of both the cross-cultural and longitudinal designs. Although the mapping of developmental trends requires complete data, at least the main guideposts are revealed in the first two years of testing. Limitations of space allow for only a few highlights to illustrate the method and some of the preliminary findings.

139

The data were organized to permit a series of analyses of variance, systematically varying five major factors of primary concern — culture, sex, father's level of occupation, initial school grade, and year of testing. Because of the importance of occupational level as a subcultural variable, the first design consisted of three major factors that were systematically varied — culture, occupational level, and year of testing; and the two remaining factors (sex and grade) were carefully balanced across the other three but could not be isolated for independent analysis. The essential features of this design, called ANOVAR I, are given in Table 2.

Table 2. Designs Used for Analysis of Two Cultures: ANOVAR I (5 Occupational Levels by 2 Years) and ANOVAR II (2 Sexes by 3 Grades by 2 Years)

Occupation of Fathers and Group No.	Texan Children			Mexican Children		
	M & F	M	F	M & F	M	F
ANOVAR I[a]						
Skilled worker	11			11		
White-collar worker	49			49		
Small businessman	21			21		
Professional man	84			84		
Large businessman	21			21		
ANOVAR II[b]						
Group I		37	37		37	37
Group II		40	40		40	40
Group III		42	42		42	42
Total	186[c]	119[d]	119[d]	186[c]	119[d]	119[d]

[a] Primary factors are balanced for sex and grade of Ss.
[b] Primary factors are balanced for occupational level of S's father.
[c] Total of 372 cases (744 scores) for combined Texan and Mexican groups.
[d] Total of 476 cases (952 scores) for combined Texan and Mexican groups.

ANOVAR I was applied to a total of 27 test scores from the HIT, the WISC, the HFD, and the OST, one score at a time, using a high speed computer. Since there were 2 scores one year apart for each test variable for 372 children, the total number of scores in each application of ANOVAR I was 744, a sufficiently large number to obtain precision in the results.

Although occupational level proved significant in a number of instances, as expected, in none was there significant interaction between occupational level and culture. Since the emphasis in this paper is upon cross-cultural developmental comparisons, it can safely be assumed that the relation between occupational level and the various cognitive, perceptual, and personality measures is identical in both cultures. Socioeconomic status, as indicated by father's occupation, does not have to be maintained in the design as a major factor isolated for analysis. Instead, it can be balanced across other factors such as sex, grade, and culture, making it possible to study systematically the interactions of these three factors and year of testing. ANOVAR II (Table 2) was designed for this purpose.

Two additional designs for analysis of variance were constructed, first by combining the upper two levels of father's occupation into one group called high socioeconomic status (SES) and the lower three levels into a second group called low SES, and then by treating the youngest children (Group I) apart from the other two age levels. ANOVAR III is a 2^4 factorial design applied to Group I only, with culture, sex, SES, and year of testing as the four factors. ANOVAR IV is a 2^5 factorial design applied to Groups II and III and contains the same factors as ANOVAR III plus one more, the grade (fourth or seventh) at time of initial testing. The two additional designs were useful for extending the analysis to those test scores available only for the youngest group or only for the two older groups. Lack of precision in matching on father's occupational level, the separate treatment of age levels, and a number of missing cases in some cells limit the usefulness of ANOVAR III and ANOVAR IV, particularly for the present discussion. Consequently, most of the results reported herein are derived from ANOVAR II, the most stable and comprehensive of the four designs.

The twenty-seven test scores which were analyzed for this preliminary report of findings in the first two years were drawn from the WISC, the Holtzman Inkblot Technique (HIT), the Human Figure Drawing (HFD), and the Object Sorting Test (OST). The seventeen inkblot scores used were Reaction Time, Rejection, Location, Form Definiteness, Form Appropriateness, Color, Shading, Movement, Pathognomic Verbalization, Integration, Human, Animal, Anatomy, Anxiety, Hostility, Barrier, and Penetration. Only Vocabulary and Block Design were employed from the WISC, since the other subtests were not given to all Ss both years. The Goodenough score for the HFD provided a well-known measure of perceptual maturity related to intelligence. Three of the scores from the OST provided measures pertinent to Gardner's "equivalence range" — number of groups into which objects are sorted, mean number of objects per group, and number of residual objects. The remaining four scores from the OST were Closed-Public %, Closed-Private %, Open-Public %, and Open-Private %, following the McGaughran-Moran scoring system.

Every one of the twenty-seven separate analyses of variance in ANOVAR II produced at least one source of variance significant beyond the .01 level.

141

In most cases, three or four components, including interactions among the primary sources, were highly significant (beyond the .001 level). Rather than present the findings one test variable at a time, as the analyses were carried out, the main results will be given according to the major factors — sex, level of father's occupation, culture, initial grade level, and year of testing, as well as the interactions among these factors. Unless otherwise noted, group differences, trends, and interactions are significant beyond the .01 level. Particular attention will be given to cross-cultural, developmental interactions because of the uniqueness of these data.

SEX DIFFERENCES

Few differences were found between boys and girls on any of the tests. As would be expected from previous studies, the performance of boys was better on Block Design, whereas girls tended to do better on Human Figure Drawing ($p = .02$). In the second year of testing on Block Design, boys showed a more marked improvement than did girls, widening still further the gap between them. Sex differences on Human Figure Drawing disappeared among the teenagers in Group III, largely because the test loses its discriminating power in older children. The mean scores level off between thirty and forty points on the Goodenough scale.

Boys received significantly higher scores than girls on Anxiety and Hostility, regardless of grade or culture. These two inkblot scores reflect the use of fear-provoking, hostile, or destructive images, symbols, and ideas in fantasy. It is not surprising that boys should exhibit more of such concepts than girls in either Mexico or the United States. The sex roles in both cultures lead one to expect more active fantasies of death, fighting, wounded people, and so forth from boys than from girls.

The most important finding is the absence of any significant interactions between sex and either culture or father's occupational level. Wherever sex differences are present, they exist equally for Mexicans and Americans and for children whose fathers work in professional occupations as well as for children from the lower classes. It is important to note, however, that in most cases sex differences in measured cognitive, perceptual, or personality functioning failed to appear, regardless of other factors.

DIFFERENCES ATTRIBUTABLE TO FATHER'S OCCUPATIONAL LEVEL

The five levels of father's occupation in ANOVAR I provide a measure of social status that is relevant in both Mexico City and Austin as an important subcultural variable. In some respects, the highly educated lawyer, doctor, teacher, or business executive in Mexico City has more in common with his counterpart in Austin than he has with the relatively uneducated blue-collar worker or clerk in his own culture. For this reason, the possible interaction of occupational level and culture in ANOVAR I is of special interest.

In none of the twenty-seven analyses of variance using ANOVAR I was the interaction between father's occupational level and culture significant, although there was a slight tendency for the Texas and Mexican children from high-status families to look more alike. At the same time, however, it should be noted that frequently both occupational level and culture proved to be significant sources of variance in their own right.

For both Mexican and American children, father's occupational level was significant for all of the intelligence tests — Vocabulary, Block Design, and Human Figure Drawing — as well as for Form Definiteness in the HIT and number of residual items in the OST. For all five scores, the significance of occupational level was due entirely to the poorer performance of children in the lowest status level, those whose fathers were blue-collar workers. Not only did these working-class children get lower scores on the three intelligence tests, but they also tended to give more vague, less form-definite responses to inkblots, and they left unused a larger number of objects when asked to construct classes of objects having common characteristics in the OST.

Perhaps more striking results would have been obtained for father's occupational level if the SES scale could have been extended downward to include children of unskilled manual workers. Unfortunately, there were not enough cases of very low occupational level available in the Austin sample to permit such an extension. Nevertheless, it is important to note the marked similarities of these findings concerning the five levels of father's occupation as they relate to cognitive, perceptual, and personality development in both cultures.

CULTURAL DIFFERENCES

Children in Mexico City and Austin differed significantly on nearly every score analyzed, and the overall results are remarkably consistent. Frequently, however, the cultural difference obtained had to be qualified by reference to the age or year tested. In thirteen of the twenty-four scores for which culture proved to be important, there was a clearly generalized cultural difference unqualified by a significant interaction. Regardless of grade level, sex, or year tested, the Mexican children received lower scores on Form Definiteness, Movement, Integration, Human, Anxiety, and Barrier from the HIT, on Vocabulary from the WISC, and on mean number of items per group, Open-Public %, and Open-Private % from the OST; at the same time the Mexicans received higher scores on Location, number of groups, and Closed-Private %.

Some insight into the meaning of these cross-cultural differences can be gained by examining more closely the nature of the variables on which the differences were uniformly obtained. A high score on Location results when a person uses smaller areas of the inkblot for his percept rather than the whole blot. Low scores on Form Definiteness, Integration, Movement, Human, and Barrier are more typical of young children than older ones. These five inkblot variables define the first factor generally found in factor-analytic studies of intercorrelations among HIT scores. A high amount of this factor is indicative of well-organized ideational activity, good imaginative capacity, and well-differentiated ego boundaries. A low number of items per group and a large number of groups on the OST reflect the same tendency to have a rather low equivalence range in classifying objects. In a similar manner, a low percentage of categorizations scored Open as opposed to Closed indicates a less abstract attitude in dealing with concepts. When taken together, these variables strongly suggest that the Mexican child is more passive in coping with the tasks set before him in the testing situation, more likely to respond in terms of his immediate sensory experience, and less likely to be highly differentiated in perceptual and cognitive structure than is the American child of the same age and social class.

In the course of actively coping with inkblots, the American child pours forth more fantasy material involving high activity (Movement) and fear-provoking images (Anxiety) than does the Mexican with his more passive style. The American child appears to be more venturesome, more willing to risk failure, freer with his fantasies, more direct and forthright in his approach.*

* As contrasted with the more passive, cautious, indirect, polite attitude considered important in Mexican interpersonal relations, the more active approach of many Americans may be responsible for their being characterized as rude and aggressive by peoples of more passive cultures, such as that of Mexico. On the other hand, the Mexican attitude, from the vantage point of a more forthright American, may be misperceived as hypocritical and lazy.

Highly significant interactions between culture and the developmental factors of grade and year were found for sixteen of the twenty-seven test scores analyzed. In some cases, these interactions were sufficiently strong to disqualify any generalized statement about cultural differences; in other cases, the differences between the Mexicans and Americans widened or narrowed with increasing age but did not disappear or reverse themselves. A few of these are discussed below in detail.

As shown in Figure 1, Reaction Time on the HIT increases fairly regularly with increasing grade level for the Mexican children, rising from a mean of 17.4 seconds for the first-graders to a mean of 20.7 for the fourth-graders and then more sharply to a mean of 25.9 for the seventh-graders. For the Texas children, however, Reaction Time starts with a mean of 15.2 seconds for the youngest group, rises sharply to a mean of 23.3 for Group II, and falls back to a mean of 19.1 for the oldest group. This inverted-V trend for the Texas children is identical to the one obtained earlier on similar samples of American children used in the standardization research for the HIT. Why is the developmental trend different for the Mexican children? Although no data are yet in hand to answer this question, one can speculate that the older Mexican child has learned to cope with novel situations (like an inkblot test) by being cautious, a characteristic consistent with the general hypothesis that Mexican children tend to have a passive coping style whereas American children are more active.

Figures 1–10 illustrate ten cross-cultural developmental trends. *Figure 1* shows the trends for Reaction Time, with the significant variance components Group, Culture by Group. *Figure 2* shows the trends for Shading, with the components Culture, Culture by Group. *Figure 3* shows the trends for Form Appropriateness, with the components Group, Culture by Group. *Figure 4* shows the trends for Penetration, with the components Culture, Group, Year, Culture by Group. *Figure 5* shows the trends for Pathognomic Verbalization, with the components Culture, Group, Culture by Year, Culture by Group by Year. *Figure 6* shows the trends for Anatomy, with the components Culture, Group, Group by Year, Culture, Culture by Group by Year. *Figure 7* shows the trends for Animal, with the components for Culture, Group, Group by Year, Culture by Group by Year. *Figure 8* shows the trends for Movement, with the components Culture, Group, Year, Culture by Group by Year. *Figure 9* shows the trends for Closed-Public %, with the components Culture, Group, Year, Culture by Group, Culture by Year, Culture by Group by Year. *Figure 10* shows the trends for Vocabulary, with the components Culture, Group, Year. The dotted lines in Figures 4–10 represent changes owing to repeated testing of the same children in the first and second years of the project.

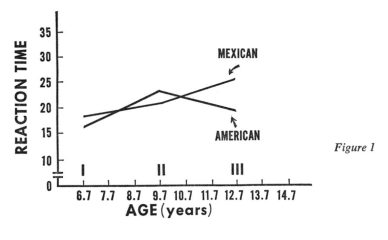

Figure 1

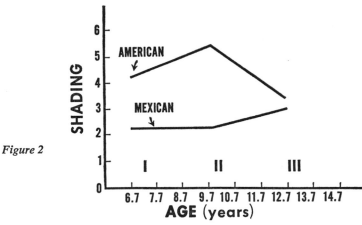

Figure 2

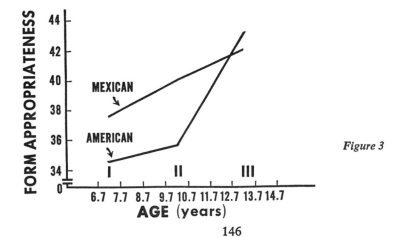

Figure 3

146

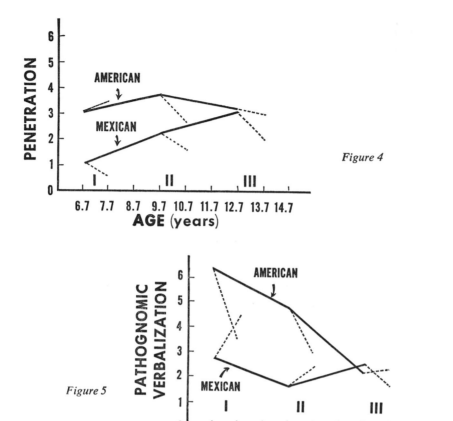

Figure 4

Figure 5

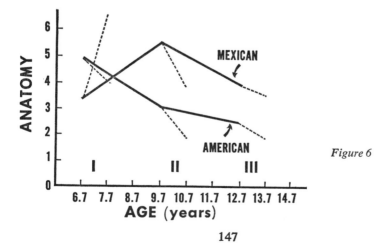

Figure 6

147

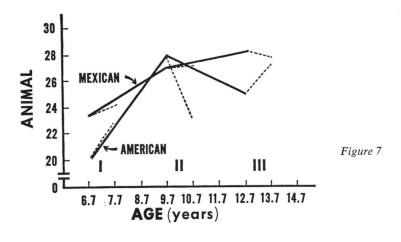

Figure 7

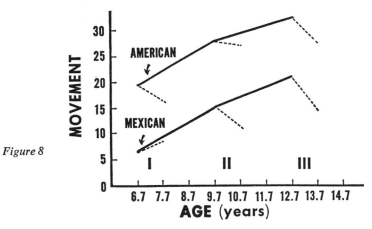

Figure 8

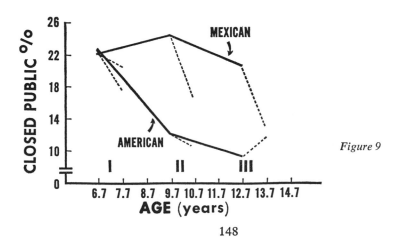

Figure 9

148

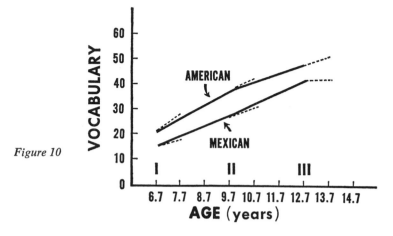

Figure 10

Being more self-confident and venturesome, the older American child reacts more quickly and still gives an acceptable response.

Shading also shows a marked interaction between culture and grade. As in the case of Reaction Time, the curve evident for Texas children in Figure 2 is identical to the one obtained for children used in the HIT standardization studies, testifying to the validity of the trend. Since the Mexican children show a slight rise from Group II and Group III, the two cultures converge in amount of Shading for the oldest group.

For Form Appropriateness, convergence of the Mexican and American children also occurs in Group III (Fig. 3). But in this case, the younger American children have significantly lower scores than the Mexican. This cultural difference in Groups I and II may result chiefly because the American children gave appreciably more whole responses (lower Location) with higher Form Definiteness, thereby increasing the likelihood that the concept would not fit the form of the blot area.

A similar cultural convergence occurs in Group III for Penetration and Pathognomic Verbalization. Although the Mexican children in Groups I and II get lower scores on Penetration, suggesting less concern with symbolic reference to disruption of the body image, the oldest group of Mexicans is similar to the oldest group of Americans (Fig. 4). The same picture holds for Pathognomic Verbalization (Fig. 5). Although the Texas first- and fourth-graders show more than twice the amount of disordered, bizarre thinking that their Mexican counterparts show, the seventh-graders are identical in both cultures. The younger Americans' higher Pathognomic Verbalization scores probably result from unsuccessful attempts

149

to integrate parts of the blot into a larger whole — attempts that produce fabulized combinations. As noted earlier, all three groups of Americans got higher mean scores on Integration than their Mexican counterparts, indicating the greater tendency of Americans to organize the parts of their percepts into larger wholes.

The highly significant triple interaction among culture, grade, and year for Pathognomic Verbalization is of special interest. Not only do the Texans and Mexicans converge developmentally in Group III, but they also converge in all three groups in the second year of testing. Inspection of Figure 5 shows that the Texan children in Groups I and II get appreciably lower scores when retested in the second year, whereas the Mexican children in these two groups get higher scores.

A triple interaction among culture, grade, and year was also found for Anatomy, Animal, Movement, and Closed-Public %, indicating that the relation among culture, age at initial testing, and effect of repeated testing is indeed complicated. These interactions are illustrated in Figures 6–9.

With the exception of scores in the first year for Group I, the Mexican children show significantly higher means on Anatomy than the Americans. For some unknown reason, there is a marked increase in Anatomy for the youngest Mexicans when tested in the second year; all other groups show a decrease in Anatomy across the two years.

For Animal, the triple interaction is even more difficult to interpret, although there is little doubt of its statistical significance. On this variable, the Mexicans show a regular progression in which scores from the second year of testing are precisely in line with expectations from the curve drawn for the three age groups. But the Texans fluctuate erratically, not only across the two years, but also across the three age groups.

The triple interaction of culture, grade, and year for Movement is illustrated in Figure 8. Here the general trend is highly regular and clearly evident. In all three groups for both years, the Texan children get considerably higher scores on Movement than do their Mexican counterparts. With the exception of the youngest Mexicans, a slight drop in Movement uniformly occurs in the second year of testing. The Mexican first-graders have so little Movement and the general developmental trend for increased Movement with age is so strong that they show an increase for the second year in spite of the practice or adaptation effect evident in the other five groups.

Figure 9 shows the same triple interaction for Closed-Public % on the

Object Sorting Test. Both Mexican and American children in the youngest group look remarkably alike. About 20 per cent of the time they give as a basis for sorting an object a response that is scored Closed-Public — for example, placing the two forks together (but excluding other silverware) and stating as a reason, "Those are both forks." The use of such concrete, specific identities as a basis for classification in the OST drops off markedly for the older American children but rises slightly for the older Mexicans. In the second year of testing, however, the two older groups of Mexican children show a much greater drop in Closed-Public % than would be expected from the general trend across the three groups.

Most of the personality, perceptual, and cognitive style variables yield complex interactions and nonlinear developmental trends across the two cultures. Generally speaking, these are difficult, if not impossible, to interpret without more data from repeated testing and analysis of intercorrelations among the many variables involved. By contrast, Vocabulary from the WISC shows a smooth linear trend across both age-grade groupings and year of testing. The apparent superiority of the Texas children, as illustrated in Figure 10, must be qualified by noting that the Spanish and English versions of the WISC Vocabulary score may not be strictly comparable. Nevertheless, it can be concluded that the course of intellectual development as measured by Vocabulary is highly regular and identical in both cultures.

DEVELOPMENTAL DIFFERENCES REFLECTED IN GRADE AND YEAR

Groups I, II, and III were carefully constructed to reflect precise control of age and initial grade in school so that developmental processes could be examined over a wide age span. Repeated testing for six years on the anniversary of the initial session will provide longitudinal data which can be merged with the cross-sectional data from the three age-groups. Since the present analysis is limited to only the first two years, any findings are admittedly tentative. Nevertheless, by assuming comparability of the three groups except for age and school grade — a reasonable assumption in view of the matching across groups on sex and level of father's occupation — some preliminary statements about gross developmental trends can be made with confidence.

All but four of the twenty-seven scores analyzed revealed highly significant components of variance owing to grade or group. Only Rejection, Location, Anxiety, and Hostility failed to show any developmental trend.

For the Holtzman Inkblot Technique, the general picture is almost identical to the age trends found in the standardization studies reported by Thorpe and Swartz (1965). Movement, Integration, and Human, the three inkblot variables which define the first factor invariably found in studies of HIT intercorrelations, show a steady increase across the three groups. A similar trend occurs for Form Appropriateness. Barrier and Form Definiteness rise steeply from first to fourth grade, leveling off thereafter. Color shows a similar trend, dropping sharply from first to fourth grade and then staying fairly constant. The remaining inkblot scores reveal different developmental trends for children in the two different cultures. These results have already been highlighted in the presentation of findings about cross-cultural differences. The Texas children remained true to form, however, in following the same patterns for these remaining inkblot variables that were observed in earlier studies of American children.

All three of the intelligence tests — Vocabulary, Block Design, and Human Figure Drawing — show regular developmental trends as expected, regardless of culture. Developmental trends are also clearly evident for the seven scores in the Object Sorting Test. The number of groups, number of residual items, and Closed-Private % tend to drop with increasing age, whereas the mean number of items per group and Open-Public % tend to increase across the three grade levels. With age, Closed-Public % falls and Open-Private % rises, but only for the American children.

Since all of the children are one year older when tested a second time, one would expect small developmental changes to be apparent in the analysis of year tested as a source of variance. Significant increases in mean scores were found for the two WISC subtests, Vocabulary and Block Design, regardless of age or culture. Similar results were found for Human Figure Drawing, but only among the American children; the Mexicans showed no change across the one year between testing sessions. For the remainder of the scores, however, either changes were not evident or their direction was the opposite of the general development trend across groups. This shift is most clearly apparent for Human, Integration, and Movement (Fig. 7) and strongly suggests the presence of practice or adaptation effects the second year. Until new data from additional repeated testing are available, it will be impossible to determine the ultimate importance of such factors in obscuring the true developmental trends.

WAYNE H. HOLTZMAN
Discussion

Given the methodological and conceptual issues outlined earlier, it is relevant to ask how well these problems, characteristic of cross-cultural, developmental research, are being resolved in the Austin–Mexico City project. Many important aspects of child development have been omitted in order to meet the stringent requirements of repeated testing in both cultures. Most of the measures currently employed have been carefully tested in both cultures to ensure their feasibility and wide-range applicability. In the later stages of the six-year testing program, an attempt is being made to strengthen the coverage of personality development by the use of parental interviews, observations of the home and family life-styles, social and behavioral data from teachers' ratings and school records, and self-inventory scales.

Special efforts have been made to eliminate or reduce substantially the influence of artifacts in the measuring process itself. Examiner variability has been minimized by intensive cross-cultural training of examiners and periodic application of quality control checks ranging from actual cross-cultural observation of examiners in action to cross-checking of scoring and coding. Preliminary standardization work was done in Mexico on minor adaptations of the Puerto Rican, Spanish version of the WISC to ensure linguistic equivalence. Only native examiners were used in both cultures, and special attention was given to possible cultural variation in response set. And yet, despite all of these precautions, the possibility still remains that a small part of the obtained cultural differences may be due either to examiners or to the contexts in which the tests were given.

Since the Austin–Mexico City project is a bicultural study in which subcultural variations play a major role, it is particularly important to examine the nature of the cultural factor and the extent to which relevant subcultural variables have been effectively matched across the two cultures. The preliminary sociological survey of the families of potential subjects in Mexico City provided the basic information needed to match Mexican school systems sampled; most of the families and their homes were remarkably similar to those of the American children. Consequently, matching on father's occupation controlled socioeconomic status, educational opportunity, and home environment well enough to ensure that the essential remaining difference between the Mexican and American children is the broad cultural one.

153

Although it is difficult to specify the major cultural dimensions on which Mexican and American societies differ, numerous informed observers have commented on this topic, and there is fairly good consensus about the dominant values, belief systems, and styles of life characteristic of the two countries. Some of the most relevant differences can be seen by comparing the traditional Mexican family with the American. A basic value in Mexico is represented by the saying, "As long as our family stays together, we are strong." As Maslow and Diaz-Guerrero (1960) have pointed out, in its solidarity, the Mexican family tends to shut itself off from the outer world. The child is brought up in the bosom of the family, playing with his siblings rather than with schoolmates or neighborhood children as the American child usually does. Unlike the father in most American families, the Mexican father is the undisputed authority on all family matters, an authority usually obeyed without question. Though she may frequently suffer in silence, the mother is revered as the primary source of affection and care. This emphasis on family affiliation leads the Mexican to say, "I will achieve mainly because of my family and for my family rather than myself." By contrast, the self-reliant American would say, "I will achieve mainly because of my ability and initiative and for myself rather than my family."

Recent studies by Peck, Angelini, Diaz-Guerrero, and Hereford (1967), by Diaz-Guerrero and Peck (1967), and by Hereford, Selz, Stenning, and Natalicio (1967) on Mexican and American schoolchildren confirm the general hypothesis that Americans tend to be more active than Mexicans in coping with the stresses of life. Although the Mexican overtly defers to authority, he prides himself on his cleverness in manipulating authority figures to achieve a goal. Most Mexicans, particularly women, subscribe to the idea that life is to be endured rather than enjoyed, that it is better to be safe than sorry, and that it is better to proceed slowly than fast. The great majority of Americans, on the other hand, seem to believe just the opposite. This bipolar pattern of values and beliefs implicit in the two cultures has been developed in a series of studies by Diaz-Guerrero (1965) as the active and passive syndromes constituting a major part of the sociocultural premises underlying American and Mexican societies, respectively.

When viewed in the light of this broad active-passive dimension distinguishing the two cultures, the results obtained thus far in the Austin–Mexico City project are easier to interpret. In general, when faced with a testing situation, the Mexican child is willing to cooperate, although he will seldom take the initiative. He will try to please the adult examiner and will tend to be cautious. By contrast, the American child will see the testing situation as a challenge to be mastered, an opportunity to show how much he can do.

To illustrate by using only the results from the inkblot scores: The American child produced faster reaction times, used larger portions of the inkblots in giving his responses, gave more definite form to his responses, and was still able to integrate more parts of the inkblots while doing so. In addition, he incorporated other stimulus properties of the inkblots, such as color and shading, into his responses more often than did the Mexican child and elaborated his responses by ascribing more movement to his percepts. In attempting to deal with all aspects of the inkblots in such an active fashion, however, he failed more often than the Mexican child. This failure is indicated by the results for such variables as Form Appropriateness, Pathognomic Verbalization, Anxiety, and Hostility. The Mexican child gave responses with better form and less often produced responses that showed deviant thinking and anxious and hostile content. Such a sweeping generalization cannot be made, though, without qualification by reference to the age or year tested. As pointed out earlier, by the age of 12.7 years the American and Mexican child converge in scores on such variables as Form Appropriateness, Shading, Pathognomic Verbalization, and Penetration. When all age levels are taken into consideration at once, however, the generalization still is a valid one. The American child tried to deal with the testing situation in a much more active fashion than the Mexican child, even when he was unable to do so successfully.

Additional evidence bearing upon the validity of the results obtained in the first two years of the Austin–Mexico City project has been provided recently by Mary Tamm (1967; see also Haroz, 1967). A unique opportunity arose at the American School in Mexico City to study both American and Mexican children attending the same classes. Tamm replicated the basic cross-cultural, test-retest design employed in the Austin–Mexico City project, using a sample of thirty first-graders, thirty fourth-graders, and thirty seventh-graders tested at exactly the same ages as in the larger study. One half of each group consisted of American children who had lived in Mexico City for at least three years before the first testing session; the other half was Mexican children. Tamm is bilingual in English and Spanish, so that she could give the tests to each child in his primary language. The Holtzman Inkblot Technique, all twelve subtests of the WISC, the Conceptual Styles Test, and Time Estimation were given initially and one year later by Tamm, who had received special training in the larger cross-cultural project.

The results obtained by Tamm for the HIT were strikingly similar to the ones reported here for the Austin-Mexico City samples. The Americans got significantly higher scores than the Mexicans on Movement, Integration, Human, Pathognomic Verbalization, Hostility, Penetration, Color, and Shading; the Americans got lower scores on Location, indicating a preference for whole responses. Developmental trends across the three age groups were almost identical with those reported here.

The only major difference in Tamm's findings and the ones presented here concerned performance on the WISC. Unlike the Austin–Mexico City results, where the Americans generally got higher scores than the Mexicans, Tamm found no difference between American and Mexican children on any of the subtests except Digit Span and Digit Symbol.

The Mexican children in Tamm's study were sent to the American School largely because their parents were achievement-oriented and wanted their children to learn English and associate with Americans. The American children went to this same school so they would become bilingual and associate closely with Mexicans. Consequently, the setting was ideal for determining which perceptual, cognitive, and personality variables are most sensitive to the basic difference in the two cultures and which are least sensitive. Since both groups of children performed essentially alike on the tests of cognitive style and intelligence — the WISC, the CST, and Time Estimation — it can be concluded that the psychological processes represented by these variables are not fundamental to the cultural factors distinguishing Mexicans and Americans. Although there may be occasional minor differences of interest, the developmental, educational, and other subcultural factors are far more important.

For the perceptual and personality variables in the HIT, however, it is apparent from Tamm's study that the cultural differences are fundamental. The magnitude of the discrepancy between the Mexicans and Americans on most inkblot scores is the same in her study and in the Austin–Mexico City project. When taken together, these results strongly suggest that something like the active-passive factor proposed by Diaz-Guerrero as fundamental to the sociocultural premises of American and Mexican life is indeed a distinguishing characteristic of the two cultures, as revealed in inkblot perception and personality.

Intriguing as they are, most of the findings from the first two years of the project must await completion of the overall longitudinal design before definite conclusions can be reached. That there are major differences in the developmental trends for Mexican and American children is clearly apparent after only two years of repeated testing. The detailed nature of these cultural differences as they shift over time in the course of development can be only dimly perceived at this point in the study. The addition of new kinds of data from parental interviews, observation, personality tests, and school performance, as well as repeated information from the core test battery should greatly enrich the opportunity to reach important conclusions about the relations of sociocultural variables to developmental processes within two major cultures.

References

Ahumada, I. R. de, R. Ahumada, & R. Díaz-Guerrero. Consideraciones acerca de la estandarización de pruebas a Latinoamérica, con ilustraciones de la adaptación del WISC a México, in C. F. Hereford & L. Natalicio, eds., *Aportaciones de la psicología a la investigación transcultural*, pp. 410–421. Mexico: Editorial F. Trillas, S.A., 1967.

Anderson, H. H., & G. L. Anderson. Social values of teachers in Rio de Janeiro, Mexico City, and Los Angeles County, California: A comparative study of teachers and children. *Journal of Social Psychology*, 1962, 58, 207–226.

Diaz-Guerrero, R. Socio-cultural and psychodynamic processes in adolescent transition and mental health, in M. & Carolyn W. Sherif. eds., *Problems of youth*, pp. 129–152. Chicago: Aldine, 1965.

——. Introduction to symposium on cross-cultural studies of personality: Cognitive and social class factors related to child development in Mexico and the U.S.A., in C. F. Hereford & L. Natalicio, eds., *Aportaciones de la psicología a la investigación transcultural*, pp. 123–129. Mexico: Editorial F. Trillas, S.A., 1967.

——, & R. F. Peck. Estilo de confrontación y aprovechamiento: Un programa de investigación. *Revista Interamericana de Psicología*, 1967, 1, 127–136.

Ervin, S. M. Language and TAT content in bilinguals. *Journal of Abnormal and Social Psychology*, 1964, 68, 500–507.

Gardner, R. W. Cognitive control principles and perceptual behavior. *Bulletin of the Menninger Clinic*, 1959, 23, 241–248.

Haroz, M. M. (Mary Tamm). El Holtzman Inkblot Test, el Wechsler Intelligence Scale for Children y otros tests en el estudio psicológico transcultural de niños de habla española e inglesa residentes en México. Ph.D. thesis, Universidad Nacional Autónoma de México, 1967.

Hereford, C. F. *Changing parental attitudes through group discussion.* Austin: University of Texas Press, 1963.

——, N. Selz, W. Stenning, & L. Natalicio. A cross-cultural comparison of the active-passive dimension of social attitudes. *Revista Interamericana de Psicología*, 1967, 1, 33–39.

Holtzman, W. H. Cross-cultural research on personality development. *Human Development*, 1965, 8, 65–86.

———. Intelligence, cognitive style, and personality: A developmental approach, in O. G. Brim, Jr., R. S. Crutchfield, & W. H. Holtzman. *Intelligence: Perspectives 1965*, pp. 1–32. New York: Harcourt, 1966.

———, D. R. Gorham, & L. J. Moran. A factor-analytic study of schizophrenic thought processes. *Journal of Abnormal and Social Psychology*, 1964, 69, 355–364.

Holtzman, W. H., J. S. Thorpe, J. D. Swartz, & E. W. Herron. *Inkblot perception and personality*. Austin: University of Texas Press, 1961.

Kagan, J., H. A. Moss, & I. E. Siegel. Psychological significance of styles of conceptualization, in J. C. Wright & J. Kagan, eds., Basic cognitive processes in children. *Monographs of the Society for Research in Child Development*, 1963, 28, 196 pp.

Kaplan, B. Cross-cultural use of projective techniques, in F. L. K. Hsu, ed., *Psychological anthropology*, pp. 235–254. Homewood, Ill.: Dorsey Press, 1961.

Lara Tapia, L., A. San Román, & R. Díaz-Guerrero. Percepción, inteligencia, formación de conceptos y cultura, in C. F. Hereford, & L. Natalicio, eds., *Aportaciones de la psicología a la investigación transcultural*, pp. 143–158. Mexico: Editorial F. Trillas, S.A., 1967.

Lindzey, G. *Projective techniques and cross-cultural research*. New York: Appleton, 1961.

McGaughran, L. S., & L. J. Moran. "Conceptual level" vs. "conceptual area" analysis of object-sorting behavior of schizophrenic and nonpsychiatric groups. *Journal of Abnormal and Social Psychology*, 1956, 52, 43–50.

Malinowski, B. *Sex and repression in savage society*. New York: Harcourt, 1927.

Maslow, A. H., & R. Diaz-Guerrero. Delinquency as a value disturbance, in J. Peatman & E. L. Hartley, eds., *Festschrift for Gardner Murphy*. New York: Harper, 1960.

Mead, Margaret. *Coming of age in Samoa*. New York: Morrow, 1928.

Moran, L. J. Generality of word-association response sets. *Psychological Monographs*, 1966, 80 (whole no. 612), 25 pp.

Moran, L., & R. Núñez. Cross-cultural similarities in association structures. *Revista Interamericana de Psicología*, 1967, 1, 1–6.

Peck, R. F., A. L. Angelini, R. Diaz-Guerrero, & C. F. Hereford. Problem solving styles in children: A cross national study, in C. F. Hereford & L. Natalicio, eds., *Aportaciones de la psicología a la investigación transcultural*, pp. 223–268. Mexico: Editorial F. Trillas, S.A., 1967.

Rosen, B. C. The achievement syndrome and economic growth in Brazil. *Social Forces*, 1964, 42, 341–354.

Rubenstein, H., & M. Aborn. Psycholinguistics. *Annual Review of Psychology*. 1960, 11, 291–322.

Sarason, S. B., K. S. Davidson, F. F. Lighthall, R. R. Waite, & B. K. Ruebush. *Anxiety in elementary school children*. New York: Wiley, 1960.

Swartz, J. D. The roles of culture, age, sex, and father's occupational level in children's responses to the Holtzman Inkblot Technique, in C. F. Hereford & L. Natalicio, eds., *Aportaciones de la psicología a la investigación transcultural*, pp. 130–142. Mexico: Editorial F. Trillas, S.A., 1967.

Tamm, Mary. Resultados preliminares de un estudio transcultural y desarrollo de la personalidad de niños mexicanos y norteamericanos, in C. F. Hereford & L. Natalicio, eds., *Aportaciones de la psicología a la investigación transcultural*, pp. 159–164. Mexico: Editorial F. Trillas, S.A., 1967.

Thorpe, J. S., & J. D. Swartz. Level of perceptual development as reflected in responses to the Holtzman Inkblot Technique. *Journal of Projective Techniques and Personality Assessment*, 1965, 29, 380–386.

Van de Castle, R. L. Development and validation of a perceptual maturity scale using figure preferences. *Journal of Consulting Psychology*, 1965, 29, 314–319.

Whiting, B. B., ed. *Six cultures: Studies in child rearing*. New York: Wiley, 1963.

Whiting, J. W. M., & I. L. Child. *Child training and personality*. New Haven: Yale University Press, 1953.

Whiting, J. W. M., & B. B. Whiting. Contributions of anthropology to the methods of studying child rearing, in P. H. Mussen, ed., *Handbook of research methods in child development*, pp. 918–944. New York: Wiley, 1960.

Witkin, H. A., R. B. Dyk, H. F. Faterson, D. R. Goodenough, & S. A. Karp. *Psychological differentiation*. New York: Wiley, 1962.

Wolf, R. The measurement of environments, in C. W. Harris, ed., *Proceedings of the 1964 invitational conference on testing problems*, pp. 93–106. Princeton, N.J.: Educational Testing Service, 1965.

LIST OF CONTRIBUTORS

List of Contributors

WANDA C. BRONSON received her Ph.D. from the University of California, Berkeley, in 1957. She subsequently joined the research staff of the Berkeley Guidance Study, and the results of some of her analyses of the longitudinal material collected in the course of that investigation are reported here. At present, she remains associated with the Institute of Human Development and is pursuing her interest in the continuity of personality by embarking on studies of development in infancy.

ROGER BROWN is Professor of Social Psychology and chairman of the Department of Social Relations at Harvard University. COURTNEY CAZDEN is an Assistant Professor in the Harvard Graduate School of Education, and Research Associate in the Department of Social Relations. URSULA BELLUGI-KLIMA is Research Associate in the Salk Institute for Biological Studies, La Jolla, California, and was formerly Senior Research Assistant in Social Relations at Harvard. The research reported in this volume is part of a longitudinal study of the development of English in three preschool children.

BETTYE M. CALDWELL attended Baylor University and the State University of Iowa, and earned her Ph.D. at Washington University. She now lives in Little Rock, Arkansas, where she maintains the editorial office of *Child Development*, of which she is editor; however, she will continue to serve as Director of the Children's Center and as Professor of Child Development and Education at Syracuse University until the fall of 1969. Her work involves participation in a multidisciplinary longitudinal study of the influence of learning environment on early child development.

MAURICE HERSHENSON received his Ph.D. from Yale University in 1963 and went directly to the University of Wisconsin in Madison, where he now is an Associate Professor of Psychology. His research is on the development of the perception of form in infants and interaction of perception and cognition in older children and adults.

WAYNE H. HOLTZMAN, Professor of Psychology and Education and Dean of the College of Education at the University of Texas at Austin, is Director in Austin of the longitudinal research project reported here. ROGELIO DIAZ-GUERRERO, Professor and Head of the Department of Experimental Psychology and Methodology at the National University of Mexico, is Director of the project in Mexico City. JON D. SWARTZ and LUIS LARA TAPIA are assistant directors of the project in Austin and Mexico City, respectively.

INDEX

Index

Active-passive coping: in Mexican compared with American child, 144, 145, 154–155, 156–157
Activity identification: APPROACH code for, 89–90
Anxiety: sex differences in, 142; cultural differences in, 144, 155, 156; absence of developmental trends in Holtzman Inkblot Technique score on, 151
APPROACH: development of, 76, 77–81; behavioral clause as unit of, 81; and types of environmental input, 95; suitability of, for idiographic study, 99; verbal-nonverbal behavior in, 101–102, 103; value of in observational research, 106–107
— behavior code: unitizing of behavior and, 81; for subject of behavioral clause, 81, 82–83, 93; for predicate of behavioral clause, 81, 83–87; for object of behavioral clause, 81, 88; for qualifiers of behavioral clause, 81, 88–89; numerical statement of, 81–82, 82–83, 83–87, 88–89; for environmental contact, 83; for attending, 83, 93, 94, 95–97, 98, 99, 100, 101; for information processing, 83–84, 95, 97, 98, 99, 100, 101, 102–104; for food behavior, 84; for manual activities, 84, 93, 94, 95–97, 99, 100, 101; for negative reinforcement, 84–85, 97, 99, 100, 101; for positive reinforcement, 85, 95, 97, 99, 100, 101; for body activities, 85–86, 93, 94, 95, 97, 99, 100, 101; for

control techniques, 87, 95, 97, 98, 99, 100, 101, 104–106
— behavior profiles: method of obtaining, 92–93; described, 93–99
— behavior record: specimen description as, 79; analysis of behavior sequences and, 79–80; method of obtaining, 80–81
— coding procedure: and description of behaviors in settings, 77; requirements for, 77–79; and analysis of behavior sequences, 78; and nonhuman objects as stimuli, 78; application of across age range, 78; and computer analysis, 78–79; ease of learning, 79; reliability of, 79
— reliability: unitizing and, 81, 91–92; among observers, 90, 91–92; among coders, 90–91, 92; for observing and coding compared, 92
— setting code: provincialism of, 89; setting alert in, 89; units in, 89; for activity identification, 89–90; for geographic region, 90; for social setting, 90
Approval-disapproval: and language development, 60, 70–71, 73; of speech, occasions for, 70; of truth value vs. grammatical correctness, 70–71. See also Reinforcement
Attending: expansions and, 63; as modal response of infant, 93; as modal response of two-year-old boy, 94, 95; not modal for two-year-old girl, 95–97; in three-year-old boy, 96–97; as modal response of four-year-old girl, 98; as

167